Praise for *The Little Book of Big Promises*

*"Promises hold powerful energy that unfulfilled or not explored can limit our potential. With **The Little Book of Big Promises**, Peggy Rometo, one of the most genuine, authentic, and caring people I know, gives us the key to unlock a treasure chest of tools to transform our pain into healing, make peace with adversity, and open the door to our true potential. Peggy is the real deal, and so is this book!"*

— **Demi Moore**

"Peggy has an extraordinary intuitive ability that could prove to be a useful resource to many."

— **Deepak Chopra**, author of *Reinventing the Body, Resurrecting the Soul*

"Peggy has been an extraordinary guide to me. With her intuitive ability, she is able to help one connect to a higher source, that which is innately in all of us but so few have the ability to access. With this book she is able to open one up to the endless possibilities of connecting to our truth and to our higher self. A gift that is immeasurable and profound."

— **Donna Karan**

"Peggy Rometo is one of the few truly kind and gentle souls that has blessed this earth. Her ability to care and genuinely understand people is a gift from the Creator. In this book, she blends her intuitive knowledge and universal truths, creating an easy to understand manual of healing."

— **Yehuda Berg**, author of *Kabbalah: The Power to Change Everything*

The Little Book of

BIG PROMISES

The Little Book of
BIG PROMISES

PEGGY ROMETO

HAY HOUSE, INC.
Carlsbad, California • New York City
London • Sydney • Johannesburg
Vancouver • Hong Kong • New Delhi

Published and distributed in the United States by: Hay House, Inc.:
www.hayhouse.com • *Published and distributed in Australia by:*
Hay House Australia Pty. Ltd.: www.hayhouse.com.au • *Published
and distributed in the United Kingdom by:* Hay House UK, Ltd.:
www.hayhouse.co.uk • *Published and distributed in the Republic
of South Africa by:* Hay House SA (Pty), Ltd.: www.hayhouse.co.za
• *Distributed in Canada by:* Raincoast: www.raincoast.com •
Published in India by: Hay House Publishers India: www.hayhouse
.co.in

Design: Tricia Breidenthal

Library of Congress Cataloging-in-Publication Data

Rometo, Peggy
   The little book of big promises / Peggy Rometo. -- 1st ed.
     p. cm.
   Includes bibliographical references.
   ISBN 978-1-4019-2453-9 (tradepaper : alk. paper) 1. Spiritual life.
2. Intuition. I. Title.
   BL624.R645 2010
   248.4--dc22

                                        2010006720

ISBN: 978-1-4019-2453-9
Digital ISBN: 978-1-4019-2931-2

13 12 11 10   5 4 3 2
1st edition, August 2010
2nd edition, October 2010

Printed in the United States of America

*To my beloved brothers, David and Larry,
of blessed memory, who if it weren't for their
passing, I wouldn't have been forced to
face my fears and embrace my gifts.*

Thank you for making me believe.

CONTENTS

INTRODUCTION

We all know what a promise means in everyday life. Promises, we might say, are our terms of engagement with the people around us—commitments we make to each other that are fulfilled by actions we take. Some of these everyday promises are small and simple: *I promise to call you over the weekend.* Some are more serious and lasting: *I promise to be faithful.* But there is another, bigger kind of promise at work in our lives—promises we make, to ourselves and to the world, about how we will live and who we will be. That's the kind of promise this book is about.

Our big promises are made before our lives even begin. They are the terms of engagement between us and the source of our life, whatever we imagine that source to be. Different people have different names for this life source—God, Allah, Buddha, Krishna, the Light, the Universe, Consciousness—and all the names are equally valid. In this book, for simplicity's sake, I use "the Creator," but you can substitute the name that means the most to you. These promises have to do with the actions, intentions, and qualities that we're meant to embody in our lives. The more we fulfill them, the more we connect with the Creator and the closer we come to the life we are meant to live. In this way, we honor the ultimate, overarching promise of our lives, which is to share who we are with the world.

The Little Book of Big Promises will teach you how to identify the promises you've made and fulfill them in your life, starting right now. The process you'll learn is simple but powerful; it's complete and full of life. It doesn't take years to perfect; many of you already have it at your fingertips, though you may not know it; and you don't need to earn it. It has already been given to you.

CHOOSING YOUR RIDE

We live between two worlds: the visible world of everyday life, where we need to eat, sleep, work, count calories, and brush our teeth; and another world that we cannot see but can learn to perceive in other ways. Most people think of the first one as the "real" world and the second as the mysterious "other side." Some people see it the other way around—the invisible world is the real one, and everyday life is the escape. And then there are those who don't believe the "other" world exists at all.

As an intuitive healer, psychic medium, and Reiki master, I work closely with the world we can't see. I believe that we not only exist in this physical dimension, called earth, but simultaneously interact in many other spiritual dimensions of reality. And I know that we are always connected to and receiving information from these other dimensions, whether we're consciously aware of it or not. For example, I receive information from sources I call "the guides" to understand what is happening in my clients' lives and create the meditations and other tools I use in my healing. I can also gain insight into a past lifetime that illuminates what's going on in this one. But it's important for you to know that if this does not fit with your worldview, you can still use the tools this book offers. You don't have to take the information you get from other dimensions literally; you can think of it as a good story that may shed a new light on your life.

If you choose to feel that you are tapping in to the information in this book entirely on your own, you are free to do so. Undoubtedly you will gain tremendous wisdom and strength for your life. But if you wish for this experience to be something grander, then just be open. Do whatever little mind trick you need to do when I bring up words or ideas you may struggle with, such as "Creator" or "past life." Don't allow them to stop you. Do your best to table your logic for now and follow the directions as they are presented in the chapters ahead. I'm not here to change your beliefs or to get you to "come over to our team." You have it in your power to achieve everything you want; you must simply be willing to let go of all that you know—just temporarily— while you are reading this book. I don't want you to take my word for it, and I don't need to have you believe me. I'm already on this path and happily engaged in fulfilling my promises. Do it for you, just to be sure. Follow through with the exercises and meditations and make your judgment at the end.

If, on the other hand, you do believe firmly in a spiritual dimension to life, but your belief is in the context of a particular faith or practice, you may fear that you'll have to abandon your faith in order to accept the ideas in this book. Far from it. The work you will do here will have the opposite effect; it will deepen your connection with your faith or with your spiritual practice. I found this out for myself shortly after I became aware of my intuitive gifts. My Catholic family was concerned about the path I was taking, and they didn't always direct their concerns to me. When a new client from my hometown didn't call me at our scheduled time, I phoned her instead, only to find out that a relative of mine, citing doubts about the "source" I might be connecting to, had told her not to talk to me! I was devastated, humiliated—and angry. After calming myself and before calling this relative, I asked for support from my guides. They gave me a beautiful metaphor that dealt with judgment and gave me the courage to continue. I'll share it with you here in case it helps you, too.

Think of the energy we call the Creator as an amusement park. Imagine you arrive in this park and you have a choice: you can go on just one of the rides, or you can try many of them. You start with the merry-go-round—maybe because it's the first ride you saw, or maybe because your family loves the merry-go-round. It really doesn't matter how you got there—it's your favorite ride! Everyone you know loves the merry-go-round as much as you do. It's safe, it doesn't go too fast, and you feel like you're in control. Well, this book lets you keep your love for the merry-go-round and try some of the other rides, too.

Perhaps you'd like to try the Ferris wheel or maybe even the bumper cars, but you're a little scared. You remember everything you have heard from your merry-go-round friends about the people who ride those kinds of rides. You can't trust them. The bumper-car people look angry and aggressive, and those Ferris-wheel people just look weird. But you have a desire, and besides, you still love everyone on the merry-go-round. You decide to try the bumper cars first, because at least you stay close to the ground, and you can run away if you don't like the ride. You have an exit strategy. So you're willing to try it—even if your best friend or family member won't. You try it because you're ready.

From the moment you step into the bumper car, you begin to feel different. Something is new here. You get your own car, and you can steer. You quickly come to understand that there are limits to where you can drive this car, but there is still a lot of freedom, unlike the merry-go-round, where you were only along for the ride. You even like the jolt you get out of being in the bumper car. You feel more awake and alive than you have in a long time. And since it's right next door to the merry-go-round, you can still see your family and friends, wave to them, and even invite them to take a spin on your new ride.

You're starting to think that maybe the Ferris-wheel people are not so weird after all and you should try that ride next. All the bumping of the cars is giving you a headache, so you decide that now is the time. Waiting in line for the Ferris wheel is the worst; you're excited but anxious. You almost get out of line because the wait is soooo long! But you stick it out. How will you ever know if you don't try it? Finally the moment arrives, and you are going higher and higher and higher. You had no idea that you could see so much from here. You can see what other people are doing and even see things that they can't see for themselves—for instance, two people coming around a corner from opposite directions about to bump into one another! Bam! Amazing. You were able to predict exactly what was going to happen from your aerial view. You can even see your family, and they can see you!

The good news is you can change rides at any time, and you've come to understand that everyone's experience of a ride is unique to him or her. It's not up to you to judge which ride people take. You may have a favorite ride now; but over the course of your life, your favorite may change, too. Best of all, all the rides are considered equal in the fairground of the Creator.

CULTIVATING TRUST

When I decided to write this book, I struggled for a long time, wondering what it was supposed to look like, whether or not I was qualified to write it, and who was going to help me. Finally, in a moment of frustration, I said, "I give up!" I stopped obsessing about the specifics—the actual writing, the particular people involved—and focused instead on thinking about what kind of book I wanted it to be, the impact I wanted it to have for people, and the kinds of people who might assist me in accomplishing it. Then I simply let go. I figured that if the Creator wanted it to happen, it would happen. I literally put the first draft of the manuscript on a shelf and forgot about it.

Weeks later, I was in the middle of a session when I suddenly felt compelled to ask my client what she did for a living. We had been working together for years, but for some reason I couldn't recall her profession. She nonchalantly announced that she was a literary agent. Then she said, "Why, do you have a book?"

I was stunned. It had happened so quickly, and it was so easy! My client had all the criteria I had asked for when I thought about the kinds of helpers I needed. By the way, her name is Cynthia Cannell. She represented me, of course, and ultimately connected me with my dream publisher, Hay House, the publisher of this book.

Writing this book and getting it into your hands was an important promise for me to fulfill, but I couldn't do it by pushing. I could only do it by letting go and trusting—trusting that my intuition was right, that I would get the help I needed, and that things would unfold as they should. Much of what you will learn in this book involves this very same kind of trust.

We throw the word *trust* around easily, but think for a moment how valuable trust is. If we could bottle it, we'd make millions overnight. If you knew unequivocally that you could trust your boyfriend forever and ever, you'd say yes and marry him. If you knew you could trust your boss, you'd give her your ideas, knowing that she wouldn't steal them from you and take the glory. If you knew you could trust your safety, you'd go out for that midnight run and enjoy the fresh air and moonlight knowing that no harm would come to you. But trust doesn't come in a bottle; we have to cultivate it for ourselves.

In this book I want to cultivate a certain type of trust, not one that is bestowed upon you because you've earned it and not one that involves blind faith, but one based on discernment: a sense or knowing that you have intuitively felt and followed by being open, aware, and patient. By listening with the tools this book lays out for you, implementing them in your life, and watching the process unfold, you will get your answer—not because I told you, or because the "guys upstairs" I work with told you, but because *it feels right and true for you*. This book is your opportunity to find that trust within you. Once you do, doors open, the earth moves, and you discover the promises of your destiny.

How to Use This Book

We make the promises that guide our lives, but we don't come into this world consciously knowing what they are. We have to reveal them for ourselves. In the chapters ahead, I'll guide you through a three-step process for uncovering a promise and bringing it into conscious awareness so you can embody it more fully and deliberately—a practice I call the Pursuit of Promises. At the end of each chapter, I will ask you to examine a significant event in your life to discover the promise it reveals. As you move through the book, the truths you uncover along the way will lead you to a fuller sense of your own purpose, helping you to discern your life's path and make a plan for moving forward.

The tools we'll use may be familiar to you, or they may be new. They include guided meditations, exercises called "energy pieces" in which I lead you through movements or self-talk to shift your subconscious, and further light work consisting of visualizations you can do on your own. From time to time, I'll ask you to listen to a guided meditation that can be found by clicking on the *Little Book of Big Promises* link on my Website www .peggyrometo.com. You'll also find the texts of these meditations in the Appendix at the back of the book. Some of the exercises involve writing down your impressions or information you receive, so you may want to get a notebook or journal that you can use to record your journey of promises.

Sometimes when you listen to a meditation, there may be parts that don't make sense to you. That's fine. Just know that section is not for you and continue listening. Conversely, if you feel I am speaking directly to you—great. I am. I hope you'll want to work with the material in this book again and again. Since we know nothing stays the same, you may discover something different or new each time you listen. Also, remember to trust that whatever you receive is accurate and applicable. There are no wrong ways of doing this.

It's fine to take someone else's experiences or passion as a starting point to help you find and experience your own truth, so from time to time I'll share stories from my clients' experiences, and I'll use examples from my own life to illustrate how the Pursuit of Promises process works. But ultimately, you must inquire on your own. This book is intended to give you a solid experience, a tangible connection with the Creator, as much as that is possible given that we're speaking about something the mind cannot really grasp. To help you develop the trust this work requires, I'll introduce you to practices for accessing information about yourself and your life that you may not even know you have available to you, using exercises that progressively deepen your connection to your intuition. Along the way, we'll look at the obstacles that get in the way of our fulfilling our promises—old patterns, beliefs, stories, and fears—and find ways to break free of these old bonds. Finally, we'll explore what you can ultimately do with the information you get about your promises, how deeply they can enrich your life and how to go on working with them once you've put this book down.

The Little Book of Big Promises is an easy, quick read, but it is formidable, too. It's for those who want to know the truth for themselves, who aren't willing to believe it without discovering and experiencing it firsthand. In other words, it's for you.

Remember, this is your journey. Make it your own, and enjoy the ride!

CHAPTER 1

A PATH OF PROMISES

*A soul without a high aim is
like a ship without a rudder.*

— E ILEEN C ADDY

In the ancient mystical text called the Zohar, Hash-em lays out for Abram the path that a human soul follows on its way into this life:

> There is a unique process of preparation that a soul undergoes prior to entering our physical realm. This process consists of promises and commitments made by the soul to the Creator. The soul pledges to embrace the spiritual path of change.[1]

But though we all start out on this path, to stay on it is another matter. As the Kabbalah scholar Rav Yehuda Ashlag has put it, "The perpetual pull and tug of the material world is of such magnitude, we forget our true purpose in life as we succumb to the illusions of physical existence."[2] To reawaken and reaffirm our soul's original commitment to walk the spiritual path is the work of a lifetime.

What exactly is the soul? As I see it, the soul is the part of you that contains the life force, or energy, of the Creator. It's the spark within you that is just like the Creator; it is eternal, and it is always connected to the origin of all life, even when you don't consciously perceive that connection.

Imagine that you are holding a glass bowl. Now imagine what happens when you drop that bowl and it shatters. Fragments of glass go everywhere, on the floor, on the counter, in your clothes. Some are up high, some are scattered low, some are larger than others, and none of the fragments are identical, but all of them are made of the same glass. I think the Big Bang was something like that—like a great glass bowl shattering—only it wasn't glass; it was the energy of the Creator. When that one great soul shattered, it created all our souls—it created mankind. That's how connected your soul, and everyone's soul, is to the Creator: they are made of the same essence, and they are part of each other. This is why, when I talk throughout this book about connecting with the Creator, I'm not asking you to look to religious doctrine; I'm talking about your direct connection to the Creator *within you.*

THE START OF THE PATH

Before entering the material world we know, each soul is born in the likeness of the Creator and awakened to its divinity. The soul makes promises to the creator to be fulfilled in the coming lifetime—much like a child going off to college and promising he will study, learn, and come home with a degree. Because we want our children to shape their own life experience, we allow them to choose their colleges, their career paths, their relationships, and so on. In the same way, the soul chooses the path of promises it will follow through the world.

When the soul leaves the spiritual dimension, its form changes from the energy of pure light and love and takes on the physical clothing of a body. This is the process of birth—your birth. Ancient mystical scholars say that an angel is with you through the entire process, even in the womb. At the moment of your birth the angel touches you just above your upper lip, creating the crease we see there. This touch, they say, makes you forget everything from the other dimension, including your promises and commitments to the Creator and the truth of your own divinity. You come into this world, this life, with the opportunity to learn all over again.

One promise we all make prior to coming into this life is the promise to reconnect with this knowledge that is concealed from us in the moment of our arrival. Imagine a box filled with the infinite possibilities of your soul, the infinite good it can accomplish here on earth. Now imagine that an amazing privilege has been extended to you: To be able to open this box and discover all the possible ways in which you can make good on these promises. To embrace it as a gift from the Creator, to open it with all the anticipation, joy, and love that you would feel if you were opening a present from your beloved.

Opening this box—bringing your promises to consciousness and to fruition—is a lifetime's work. The actions you take and the things that happen to you in your physical reality are reflections of the promises you made before entering this life, and these promises are awakened one by one as your awareness expands. Your life circumstances are designed to propel you along your path of promises and wake you up once again to your divinity.

WAKING UP

Sometimes we don't see our circumstances that way. We may come to believe that our pain is real and binding and cannot be fixed. When this happens, we lose touch with the Creator's presence in our life, and we lose touch with our promises; we become convinced that the pain in our life has more power and allure than the fulfillment we will experience by following through on our promises.

If for some reason we are not in touch with our promises, it is only because we have disconnected by choice, consciously or otherwise. It's our ego, the controlling and self-serving part of us, that brings this about; it drags us down, convinces us that we're victims, or makes us think we can walk the path alone. Our ego also makes other destructive and divisive choices for us about whom we can and cannot trust, including ourselves. For instance, are you afraid that you will make a mistake or make the wrong choice with your career, life partner, or business partner? Do you worry or create unnecessary fear in your life? All of these things happen when we somehow allow our ego to disconnect us from the Creator—which is the same thing as getting disconnected from the all-knowing part of ourselves. Are we really disconnected? No. It is just like a cloud covering up the sun. The sun is still there, even though we can't see it. If we stop and pay attention, we may be able to feel its warmth. And when the clouds move, we are able to see the sun again.

A little later on, we'll take a closer look at the workings of the ego and the various obstacles it can put in your way. For now, just know that ultimately you have the power of choice. You can choose to overcome those obstacles and restore the lost connection by making the decision to serve a higher power: your inner knowing, rather than your ego; your whole soul, rather than just your mind. When you achieve this level of connection, you will be freer than you ever imagined. You will be able to light the heavens with your creativity and the earth with your accomplishments. You will ignite a passion and power within you that not even the strongest foe can surmount. And none of this will diminish your mind: on the contrary, you will want to use it to validate your experiences. It's just that you will no longer be confined by the logic of your mind or by your ego's desires in the physical realm. You won't want to pay that kind of attention to your ego anymore; you'll be more interested in listening for the authentic voice that you will come to recognize as your own.

At a certain point, you will discover that you are being led with more than your own intuition. You will be blessed everywhere with signs from the Creator, and the path will open up without struggle. Once you are on this path, there is no challenge too big or too small to take on. You start to welcome the "down" times so that you can make the effort to break through the obstacles in your way, because you know that when you do, the air will clear and a new sign will appear. You learn to ride these waves with anticipation and excitement. You learn to run after the worst aspects of your ego and subdue them so you can reveal ever bigger promises.

And you start to respond to an even higher calling—to engage and embrace promises on a level beyond your individual life so you can help the whole world along its path to unity. These are Universal Promises, and we'll talk more about them in Chapter 8. But first, let's look at the process you will use to uncover and reveal the promises on *your* path.

THE PURSUIT OF PROMISES

The Pursuit of Promises is a process I've been given to help you look back over your life and reflect on the turning points in it—the events that have been most significant for you. These pivotal moments are the places where your promises to the Creator are revealed. The events may be tragic or joyful; they may be places where we feel, looking back, that we chose the wrong path; or they may simply be opportunities to learn lessons about life. They may be dramatic—a birth or a death, a relationship starting or ending, a job loss or a major move, even a supernatural experience—or as simple as a conversation that helps us see something in a new light. Whatever these events consist of, they are crossroads where we find signposts that help us determine our best next step. They create a new conversation within us that draws us closer to our destiny.

The Pursuit of Promises process asks you to answer three questions about each experience in order to bring its promise to light:

- *Describe an event that changed the direction of your life.*

- *What did you come to desire because of this event?*

- *What promise did this experience reveal?*

At the end of the first nine chapters in this book, I'll ask you to uncover the promise of one important event. I'll include examples from my own experience to show you how the process works, followed by some space for you to reflect on the turning points in *your* life.

Before you start, it's a good idea to list all the events you're going to examine. So sit down and make a list of nine significant experiences. Go back as far as you can and arrange them in the order in which they happened. It doesn't matter if these events are clustered together or evenly spaced: you may find five turning points between the ages of 10 and 20 and then nothing until age 35, or vice versa. If it helps you to start with the most recent event and then work backward, that's fine, too. Once you've made your list, you'll use the earliest event first and work forward, saving the most recent event for Chapter 9.

Discerning Your Direction

Each turning point in our life, each of our promises, shapes us a bit more—each one brings forth a piece of us that we need. And each one points the way to the next. As you work through the Pursuit of Promises process, what you're doing is looking back at the road you have traveled and discerning the signposts that you followed—knowingly or unknowingly—to get to where you are today.

Along the way, you should start to see a direction, a theme, emerging as you notice the connections between one event and the next. These connections can offer clues to your life's greater purpose, as we'll see in a later chapter. When you come to your ninth turning point, you'll be revealing your *current* promise, the one you are working on in your life right now. Then, in the tenth and last chapter, I'll show you how to turn that promise around and determine for yourself the next step on your path. You'll use your current promise to set a specific goal that will allow you to actively embody that promise, fulfill it, and carry it forward in your life. When you do this, you tap directly into the energy of the Creator. Now you're no longer just experiencing the effects of outside forces at work on you—you're becoming your own cause.

Please don't skip doing the Pursuit of Promises. You'll need the information it gives you for the exercises at the end of the book, and it will lead you to greater insights about your life and who you are. In fact, my hope is that you'll get so much out of it that you'll come back to this book every year, focusing on nine life-altering events that have occurred for you *during the year* since the last time you went through the process. Doing this exercise on an annual basis will help you stick closer to your life's path and the fulfillment of your promises.

Those three questions are the key to seeing what you've accomplished, where you've come from, and how far you've come. And, like any exercise, the more you do it, the more you're building your muscle. After you work out for a month or six weeks or eight weeks, your body becomes accustomed to the new movements and starts to get stronger. It's the same way with the pathways in your brain. Once you've gone through this book and done the Pursuit of Promises exercise nine times, you'll start to get good at it. You'll say, *Okay, I know what I'm doing—I see how this event came about, and I understand what the outcome is telling me.*

I can't overstate the importance of examining these events, because they take place specifically to awaken us to our potential. They happen so we can get an ever more refined sense of who we are. They take us from being the coal to being the diamond. When the events are challenging, it's all the more important to welcome the difficulty, to meet it head on. The more you try to run away from a really big issue or shrink from dealing with it, the more it haunts you. It's an energy drain, it's exhausting, and you're just dragging out the lesson that you're bound to learn in the end. So if your house burns down, or you find your spouse is cheating on you, or you lose your job, that life-changing event is there to show you what you're made of. And if the stuff you're made of isn't yet enough to meet the challenge, then finding your way through it is an opportunity to grow.

My Promise

The easiest way for me to explain how the Pursuit of Promises process works is to describe for you exactly how I applied the three questions to an event in my own life. In each of the chapters ahead, I'll give you an example from my path, but here, I'll tell you the full story.

Describe an event that changed the direction of your life.

When I was 24, I dreamed that my brother David, who was 28, died in a car accident. Several weeks later, David really was killed in a car accident on his way to work, just as I had dreamed.

I was living in Florida at the time, and David had been living in Iowa. When I got back to Florida after his funeral, I lost the apartment where I'd been living and had to move into a new place that was virtually empty. I felt like a cross between a walking zombie and an emotional wreck. It's weird when a loved one who lived somewhere else dies—it's almost like it didn't happen. No one really knows you have suffered a loss. You go to work, you come home, you go to the store, run errands, or work out; and there isn't anyone stopping you to ask if you're okay. I felt that all I had left was God, so I did the only thing I knew to do. I tried to talk to God.

At the time, I was still practicing the Catholicism of my childhood, so I prayed in the only way I knew how. I grabbed a Bible I'd had since high school, took my rosary in the other hand, and sat down on the floor in the middle of my empty new living room. I decided to let God speak to me by whatever passage I opened to; I would know those were the words I needed in that moment. So I opened the Bible and began to read. I don't even remember what the passage was about—all I remember is the tremendous energy and love that I suddenly felt pouring into my body. I'll tell you some more about this energetic experience, my first ever, a little later on. For now, I'll just say that the experience allowed me to completely let go of my anger at losing Dave. The energy I felt was so filling that I could not possibly want for anything. It took away my fear and pain and replaced it with unconditional love, which I'm certain Dave was part of.

What did you come to desire because of this event?

This question is about how you felt at the time the event took place. As you reflect on your turning points, try to remember the emotions you experienced at that time, not how you feel about the event today. Try to go back to the root of the emotion. In my example, I was in so much pain that what I desired above all was to be out of pain. I also desired to be reconnected with my brother, to talk to him again, to feel his presence again. And I wanted the whole world to experience the feeling of unconditional love that I felt that day.

Desire is a wakening within your spirit. Desire is the key to everything, because if you don't have desire you won't do anything. I wouldn't have gotten myself out of pain without the desire to do so. Ultimately, for me, it was really about the desire for peace of mind.

What promise did this experience reveal?

How do you make the leap from describing the experience and identifying the desire to revealing the promise? Basically, the promise reflects the way you felt after you came through this event. It takes the form of a statement that equates to that feeling. So after I regained my peace of mind—after I went through that experience and actually felt the peace of mind reflecting back—my promise was revealed as: *I am Peace.*

Another way to think of this promise is as a kind of mantra. Mantras are healing phrases that we can use to shift the way we're feeling. The words actually carry a vibration that causes a shift in the body at both the physical and the spiritual level. Mantras are the antithesis of the way we're feeling in a given situation; they're the antidote. When we say the words out loud, they bring up all the emotion we want to be rid of. It's a way of moving that emotion out of your body and exchanging it for its opposite. And "I am" is a very powerful form for a mantra to take. Saying "I am *at peace*" makes it sound as if you're addressing just one little piece of your life. When you say, "I am Peace," you're embodying the essence of peace completely.

So do you feel like peace after your brother has died? Did I? No. But if I had said, "I am Peace," even though I wasn't, it would have brought my grief to the surface to be released, much the way my energetic experience did, and gradually exchanged it for peace until eventually I really did feel at peace. At some point, after several weeks, if I were to continue to say that phrase, there would be no reaction, no grief coming up. I would just feel that sense of peace. The antidote would be working.

Sometimes it's difficult to put into words what helped you get through an experience, what promise it revealed. If that happens to you, don't worry—this is where your intuition can help you. Just say, "Okay, I'm going to pick a number from 1 to 72." Then turn to page 147 and look up the mantra—the "I am" promise—that corresponds to the number you picked. The number will correspond with a mantra that is likely to help illuminate that period in your life. Use that mantra to answer the third question—*What promise did this experience reveal?*—and simply trust that it's right for you.

✑THE PURSUIT OF PROMISES✑

Peggy's First Example

Describe an event that changed the direction of your life.

In 1984, I had a dream that my 28-year-old brother David would be killed in a car accident. Several weeks later, just as I had dreamed, David died in a car accident on his way to work. Weeks later, while praying, I had an energetic experience that completely took away my fear and pain and let me feel unconditional love, which I'm certain Dave was part of.

What did you come to desire because of this event?

I wanted peace of mind, release from my pain, and to be with Dave just one more time. I wanted the entire world to experience the same feelings of unconditional love that I felt that day.

What promise did this experience reveal?

I am Peace.

Your First Promise

Describe an event that changed the direction of your life.

What did you come to desire because of this event?

What promise did this experience reveal?

CHAPTER 2

THE POINT
OF ORIGIN

The intuitive mind is a sacred gift and the rational
mind is a faithful servant. We have created a society
that honors the servant and has forgotten the gift.

— ALBERT EINSTEIN

Have you ever been tongue-tied? Have you ever
wanted to express yourself but failed to find the words?
You may have to go back to junior high to remember
what that felt like, or it may have happened just a few
weeks ago on a date or a job interview. Or maybe you're
at the other extreme—a Chatty Cathy who talks nonstop
or one of those people who consider themselves authori-
ties on everything and give long speeches to prove it.

Both these modes of expression block the truth.
Awkward silence suppresses what's real, and superfluous
words drown it out. The tongue-tied kid doesn't want it
to be known that he feels insecure; the Chatty Cathy is
overcompensating because she's insecure, too. Even the
arrogant person who is doing all the talking just wants
to prove she's smart.

You've probably been in one or the other of these
positions at some point in your life, and you may have

been in both. But now think about what it's like when you're *not*—when the words flow and you're saying exactly what you want to say without even trying. Your thoughts stop racing and your mind slows down; you feel more grounded and more secure in who you are; you relax and start to trust the flow of life. You somehow start to say the right thing at the right time, and you know when it's best to say nothing at all.

The ability to slow down, let go, and trust the flow is a key element in being able to uncover your promises. It's the first step in tapping into the vast wealth of information that your intuition can help you access. This chapter is about helping you enter that space of trust and right timing, the space where the soul and the Creator meet, and learn to draw from the wisdom it offers.

A SPACE OF TRUST

There is a field of energy between the Creator and the soul, a still point of perfect trust and infinite possibility that allows creation to occur. I call this space the *Point of Origin*. We have access to this space at all times, whether we know it or not; our souls are always connected to it. It holds our promises, our purpose, and the answers to all our questions.

Science has proven to us that everything is energy. The tables, chairs, and walls that we see are all made up of small particles that are moving and fluid and only appear to be solid. The same is true of human beings. Our soul is pure energy, and it is always connected across all dimensions; it always has access to the Point of Origin, where it interacts moment to moment with the Creator.

It recharges and refuels automatically, just as the heart beats without the mind consciously telling it to.

Many of us first become aware of connecting with the Point of Origin in sleep states—not only in prophetic dreams but also when we get glimpses of the answers we are seeking to our current life problems. Then we begin to notice it during our waking hours in the form of a quick intuitive flash, a moment of knowing. We sense the power of these interactions, and we start to look for more openings into this space. Finally, we are able to summon it at will and to be fully present to it. It is the space between our logic and our intuition, our fears and our knowledge, our habits and our triumphs, our questions and our answers. It's the space between our loneliness and our true love. It is a space of nothingness where everything is possible.

Some of us can access this space more readily than others. Gifted writers, artists, musicians, actors, and comedians all tap into this space to access the abilities for which they're celebrated. So do experts in other, less readily accepted fields—psychics, mediums, faith healers, and all those who use their "sixth sense" (which is just another name for intuition) to express themselves in the world. Some people are so terrified of "hearing" anything that they shrink from interaction with "those types." Maybe you've felt this way yourself. However, if you were to have a conversation with a reputable individual in one of these fields, and you could listen not with your critical faculties but with your gut instincts, your inner knowing, you probably wouldn't be nervous at all. You would see the value of this person's knowledge and skill, just as you do with your accountant, lawyer, or doctor. In fact, you'd probably want to find a way to use his or her gifts to get answers in your life. If you're reading this book, you are most likely looking to cut out the middleman and reveal those answers for yourself. Bravo! You won't be disappointed.

THE POINT OF ORIGIN IN YOUR LIFE

As I've said, everyone connects with the Point of Origin, including you. Anytime you get a flash of brilliance or a feeling about someone or something that turns out to be right, you are accessing this all-knowing place. Most people think it's purely their brains or good luck that gives them that million-dollar idea and the ability to realize it. You might even hear someone say, "I thought of it out of the blue!" Perhaps the next time you hear that—or say it yourself—you'll realize that "the blue" is really the Point of Origin.

I believe that all of the answers we will ever need throughout our lives have been answered for us even before we think to ask the questions. These answers await us in the Point of Origin space, and all we need to do to access them is to ask the right questions. In the upcoming chapters, you'll learn how to tap into this space more consistently; and by doing so, you'll have more certainty in all areas of your life. You'll become more creative and confident. People will be drawn to your certainty, and they will value more of what you have to say, all because of this ability to let go and trust.

If you already experience this connection naturally and readily, the way artists and psychics do, a good way to cultivate it is simply to sit down and let your inner knowledge pour out of you, whether you're developing a creative idea or working on the Pursuit of Promises process in this book. Don't judge what comes up, just allow yourself to communicate it. If you have difficulty with this, pretend you're psychic! Ask yourself, *If I were psychic, what would I say?* Then just let the information flow. In other words, trust the process and yourself.

To create something new, you must go through different stages. First you get an infusion of energy that comes from touching on an exciting idea; you see the seeds of a dream and start to sense that it can become real. Then doubt may creep in, perhaps because you know others may have the same idea or because fears of loss arise. But if you have a strong desire and you know you can be successful by staying focused and true to your path, you will get there someday.

Let's explore this possible future by returning to your childhood, a time when your soul's knowledge of its purpose in being born into this world was still fresh, not a distant memory. What was your dream as a child? What games did you play? Did you see yourself traveling the world? Did you see yourself as a star athlete? Did you want to help people? As you allow yourself to recall your dreams, feel yourself connecting with this part of the child that you still carry. For example, when I was a child I often played detective games, told ghost stories, and held spooky séances with my cousins. I loved to write and to read books. I loved any activity that involved solving a mystery or finding an answer. We've all had this playfulness, a natural curiosity about things, and simply taking a few minutes to reflect on that period in our lives opens the door to what attracted us then. It doesn't mean you'll go back and do the things you dreamed of or played at, although you may; it is more about tapping back into that energy, reviving your connection with your hopes, your desire, and your intuition. It's simply that reconnecting with the pure potential you had as a child, when you knew no limits, is essential to creating the desire you need in your life now to uncover your promises and fulfill your purpose.

Sometimes it requires hard work, and there may be periods of struggle. Yet there will be rewards along the way, and you'll see progress. You must be willing to let personal gain take a backseat—just for the moment. Externally, it may look like you aren't even close to achieving your goals or doing what you want to do in the world. You may be in what looks like a no-win situation, such as taking care of an aged parent and putting your own life on hold. But what if you are looking for your soul mate and that person turns out to be your mother's doctor? Or maybe you've lost your six-figure job and gone to work at Starbucks, just to keep some money coming in, when a million-dollar idea for the chain hits you over the head and propels you up the corporate ladder. That's what I call trusting the process.

ACCESSING THE POINT OF ORIGIN

You can connect with the Point of Origin at any time, and you already do so without knowing it, as we've seen. But some of us need additional support to understand this flow of energy or believe in our ability to access it. So now, to get you started, I'll offer you some basic instructions that you can use throughout the book. You can go deeper into the process, if you so desire, using the tools you'll find in Chapter 5 and Chapter 9.

Accessing the information stored at the Point of Origin is a journey of self-discovery that calls on our intuition, our focus, and our trust—and all these tools are at our disposal through the simple use of our breath. Here's a simple and effective method you can use to connect. Close your eyes and tip your head down slightly toward your chest to signal that you are looking inward. Imagine that the center of the earth is located deep beneath your feet. Where that spot is, imagine placing a special trinket or sign—anything from a large X to a beautiful colored stone to an actual welcome mat that may pop up in your imagination. Now take in a deep breath while imagining that from that spot a tunnel of white light has opened up. As you inhale, drawing your breath up through the center of your body, you are bringing that tunnel of white light up through you. Inhale until you get to the top of your head, hold your breath for three seconds, and then exhale, this time focusing on sending your breath and the white light back down through the inside of your body all the way to the center of the earth, relaxing your body and your breath as you go down. Do this for at least three complete cycles of breaths.

In the beginning, I found it helpful to open my mouth to exhale as I was relaxing and moving the tunnel of light back down my body. I used an anchor as my symbol, to represent tying me to the center of the earth, since this entire process is about grounding us and helping us become present. By pretending to create the tunnel of white light, you are giving your mind something to do while your sixth sense works.

After completing the cycle of three breaths, you can now ask yourself a specific question about anything you are trying to discern. This might be the promise revealed by one of your turning-point experiences, or it might be a question about your relationship or work situation. And this is the process that you will use over and over again throughout this book and in your life. It's a simple method that enables you to receive information through a conduit that can override logic, sidestep your conscious awareness, and tap into the mysteries of the universe.

Now, before we go any further, I would like to take you on a conscious journey—one that will connect you with your deepest feelings of inner knowing and make it easier for you to trust the process that will unfold as you do the exercises in this book. This is the same trust that was yours before you came into this life, a trust so deep and pure that it resonated throughout your being. No words were necessary to convey the depth of love you felt from and for the Creator. Your breath was the same breath, your heartbeat the same tempo, your voice the same tone as the Creator's. In this exercise, you can taste that oneness and that trust again.

The Meditation Process

To do the meditations in this book, it's best to find a quiet place and set aside time when you won't be disturbed. Make sure you have pen and paper handy to write down what you experience. Then relax and get comfortable. You can do the meditations sitting in a chair or lying down—it doesn't matter. (It's just not a good idea to do them while you're driving!) Don't be discouraged if you fall asleep. Trust that your subconscious is getting what it needs.

Some of the exercises are a bit like the children's game Simon Says: I'll say something and then give you time to repeat it, preferably out loud. I will use the phrase "I give myself permission" as a cue for you to repeat that whole phrase—for example, "I give myself permission to excel beyond belief."

As you go into the meditation work, be aware that you may experience powerful emotions—tears, anger, memories. Don't worry, and don't try to stop the feelings; they're just coming up to be released. Simply trust the process and remember these meditations are taking you one step closer to revealing your promises!

·················· *Suitcase Meditation* ··················

The following exercise will help you learn to relax and trust the process in order to access the information that's available to you but hidden. It's your first opportunity to trust what you receive via your intuition, if only so you can see what happens when you do. This meditation will give you a chance to get back in touch with the knowledge you brought into this world, even if it's only a glimpse—to answer the big questions: *Why am I here? What am I supposed to accomplish? How will I do it and who will help me?*

When you're ready, go to www.peggyrometo.com and listen to "Suitcase Meditation." At the end of the meditation you'll be given a short period of silence to continue to observe your experience before I give additional directions.

Go ahead and listen to the meditation now. Then come back to this section.

Now that you've listened to the Suitcase Meditation, you can begin to write about your experience. This might take the form of memories that came up during the meditation, pictures or words that came to mind, emotions you felt, or sensations in your body. Trust your experience and allow it to take shape; do not question it, do not edit it, do not try to control it or direct it. Just allow it to flow, as if you are lying in a stream and the water is washing over you. You're simply observing your experience now.

It's important to reestablish this connection, because at the time of our birth we still have full knowledge of our purpose in coming into this world, at this time, with this family, in this place on the planet. The timing and perfection of those choices influence how we should proceed now to discover and fulfill our destiny.

I am not saying that you don't have free will or that you are born into a life that is already scripted. To a degree it is—the players have been named—but the words, the script, and the path are yours to create. It's your journey—and the answers you rediscover in the Point of Origin can help guide you on the way.

⦵THE PURSUIT OF PROMISES⦵

Peggy's Second Example

Describe an event that changed the direction of your life.

In 1998, another of my brothers, Larry, was killed in a horrific accident. Unlike my first brother's death, this one came with no warning to me. Driving to Larry's funeral in Iowa from my home in Kansas City with my three-month-old daughter in her car seat, I sobbed, begging God to let me see my brother one more time: *Please, please, please, let him come back to me so I can say good-bye.*

Over the next three days, I had visitations from both of my brothers that changed my life. I smelled the cologne that Larry always wore. I channeled automatic writing from Dave. I had a dream—really an out-of-body experience—in which I saw them both, and they reassured me that they were together. They even told me how to find items I had lost, and they were right.

So, for the first time, I started to receive information from other dimensions. I started to feel connected to people I knew who had died; I was hearing things from them, and the things I was hearing were coming true.

What did you come to desire because of this event?

I wanted to understand how I had been able to communicate with my brothers so I could do it again and again. I wanted to be able to help others have this same experience so they could feel the same joy and peace I did. And, as time went on, I wanted to understand what my life was to be used for—I wanted to receive a sign and connect with my purpose.

What promise did this experience reveal?

I am Connected.

Your Second Promise

Describe an event that changed the direction of your life.

What did you come to desire because of this event?

What promise did this experience reveal?

CHAPTER 3

CREATING YOUR REALITY

A loving person lives in a loving world.
A hostile person lives in a hostile world.
Everyone you meet is your mirror.

— KEN KEYES, JR.,
HANDBOOK TO HIGHER CONSCIOUSNESS

When you connect to the Point of Origin, you are uncovering the purpose and the promises you brought into this world. In a sense, you're uncovering *yourself*—reconnecting with your best and truest self.

More than a decade ago, when I spontaneously began receiving information and insight from the guides, I was curious to know how things work on the other side. What goes on there? How is it set up? It was explained to me that there are different dimensions to the universe and that we exist in all the dimensions at once. In the highest of these dimensions is our most perfected self. There is no lack there, only the pure perfection of the soul. As we work in the physical dimension, our current reality, to uncover and embody our promises, we are making room for our perfected self to manifest in our physical reality.

This wasn't the first time I had heard of the soul's perfection. I had received the knowledge that our souls are perfect years before, in Catholic grade school and high school. The difference was that back then, we were taught that we could access this perfection only in Heaven after we died—and only if we were good—and, even then, only after an obligatory stint in Purgatory that would make our souls pure enough for union with God. Later, I came to understand that through our actions and our desire to connect to the Creator, we can reach perfection here, on this earth, in this life. I know now that this is the ultimate goal of the soul.

EGO AND FEAR

If this connection is really available to us in our current reality, why don't we all live as our best and most perfect selves? What comes between us and our perfection? It's simply our controlling, self-serving ego, the part of us that is opposed to spirit and works to contract rather than expand.

The ego keeps us from believing that we can achieve perfection at all, because it buys into the notion that our current reality is all there is. But this reality is *not* all there is, just as your ego is not all you are. When you let go of your doubts, insecurities, prejudices, and judgments—even if it's just for a moment—you transcend your ego's limits and reconnect with who you really are and why you are here. When you let go of your pain and your fear, you can bring your promises within reach.

In our physical reality, we have a natural inclination to receive from others. Our job is to overcome our selfish desires and get as close to the Creator as we can. A few of you may be shaking your head and saying, "That's not true. I like to give to people. I like to do things for others." Why do you like to give to others? Because it makes you *feel* good, or you want them to like you, or it may score you brownie points with someone else. The list goes on. In every case, you are still receiving something. There is no action we take that we don't get something out of, not one. Even when we love unconditionally, we are receiving a reflection of this love back. We're still in receiving mode. At least this seemingly "selfless love" is a higher form of love and can help others give the same; the point is to not fool ourselves into thinking that we are noble or pious because of the goodness we share with others. Though loving in this way nurtures the soul, it nurtures the ego, too.

The Stories of Your Life

Much of the time, ego is about looking good. Sometimes when you're working on pursuing your promises, you have to attack a problem, and it's messy—which doesn't look good. The ego doesn't want to be caught not having the right answers, and it hates not knowing how things will turn out. So it discourages you from trusting your intuition, really looking at yourself, and doing what you need to do to live your own authentic life.

This discouragement can take a number of forms: patterns that keep us stuck in destructive behavior or painful emotion, beliefs that no longer serve us, fears that hold us back, or negative self-talk that weighs us down. Or it can show up as stories we're caught up in reliving—things that happened to us earlier in our life-time, or things that we've carried with us from other dimensions, other lives.

If it's hard for you to grasp the idea that other di-mensions exist simultaneously with this one, or to be-lieve in past lives and their influence on us now, that's fine. Just think of them as stories that influence us, for better or worse. You can imagine that some of these sto-ries have better endings than others. The stories with good endings don't cause us emotional or physical prob-lems now, but the stories in which we don't fare so well create blocks or challenges for us, either physically or mentally, in our current reality. As an example, let's say in one story (or dimension or past life) you drowned: consequently you're now terrified of water.

Sometimes these stories connect not only to your emotions, like a fear of water, but also to your character—the kind of person you are. For example, if you were a thief in another lifetime and never got caught, you might now have a penchant to shoplift or to steal and not think too much of it. Or you might suspect others of stealing from you, experience a lack of trust around your own possessions, or go through cycles of loss. Whatever the source of these stories, the benefits of releasing the blocks they create are endless. The more time and en-ergy you put into shifting your stories—releasing your fears, phobias, anger, and other automatic negative re-sponses—the more you'll begin to see changes in your personality, anything from becoming more trusting to becoming more outspoken or outgoing. You'll no longer turn to your negative behavior as an automatic reaction to your environment. You'll begin to attract the right people, places, and situations to assist you in revealing and sharing your gifts in the world. Your life will become better because you're living the life you were meant to live, not some old story that no longer defines you.

Seeing Your Patterns

Sometimes an old story locks you into a destructive way of behaving, like the former thief who falls into shoplifting—a role that you're stuck in, a theme that recurs in your life, or a label you put on yourself. Look at the list below and see what jumps out at you. Write it down. I encourage you to do this because it's really effective in breaking the patterns that hold you back.

You may find that you have more than one theme, or that you play some role that's not on this list. If so, write down your own, whatever seems fitting to you. Again, you do not have to actually believe that other dimensions exist or that previous lives influence us today. Rather, you can simply think of your current circumstances as a "good story" that needs a different ending for you to be successful.

Please don't be offended by these labels—the grittier, more real, and more intense the names you give these roles you play, the easier they become to spot.

Arrogant Bitch	Martyr
Bastard	Victim
Miser	Bully
Whore	Thief
Molester	Crook
Drunk	Mismatcher (always contradicting)

Fat Slob	Idiot
Nervous Nellie/Ned	Selfish Pig
Compulsive Gambler	Drama Queen
Bigot	Loser
Critic	Know-It-All
People Pleaser	Killjoy
Control Freak	Racist

So how do these labels play out in our lives? Often they form the backbone of our negative self-talk. We may have thoughts about ourselves that use these words and phrases: *I'm such a cheap bastard* or *I'm such an idiot* or *I'm so mean, insensitive, jealous, etc.* The list goes on and on, and because we believe what we say to ourselves, it becomes our reality. That self-talk gets recorded in our minds and bodies, whether it's over a few months or over a lifetime, and we play the same record over and over again.

If no role springs to mind and you're having trouble pinning down the theme of your negative self-talk, try asking yourself this question: *What is the one thing that I would absolutely hate to be called?* Think of a name you would find so deeply humiliating that you couldn't stand it if someone thought of you that way. Try this now. Just write down one phrase that you would rather die than find yourself labeled. Don't go any further until you do this.

Once you've written down the last thing you'd want to be called, the next step is to ask the Creator to bring this trait to your attention wherever it appears in your life. The point is to help you identify the unconscious behavior so you can become conscious of it and thereby break its hold on you. We're trying to scratch that old record so it can't go on playing automatically and keep you reacting in negative ways.

To give you an example, when I asked myself this question, I wrote down "Arrogant Bitch." This was back in my late 20s, and I remember thinking, *There is NO WAY I'm that.* I was feeling rather smug about it, too, I might add. But I really discovered my Arrogant Bitch after asking the Creator to give me a sign that would show it to me. I remember standing in a checkout line and getting indignant with the sales clerk, acting impatient, challenging her, being every inch the arrogant bitch. And then, boom, I heard that phrase in my head. *Here's that arrogant bitch!* I was shocked, and then immediately I tried to push that emotion away, which only made it worse. I was so ashamed, I slinked out of that store with my tail between my legs.

In order to change your theme, you must first recognize it so when this behavior comes up you'll be able to embrace it—the prerequisite for letting it go. In the checkout line, I struggled with the energy and made it worse. Instead, when you experience this negative behavior or energy, embrace it: say to yourself, just as a friend might observe it for you, "Hey, there's me being (fill in the blank—a cheap bastard, a bigot, a fat slob)." Don't push it away. Relax into the feeling. As soon as you acknowledge and embrace the label without struggle or an attempt to change it, the energy simply dissipates. It's remarkably quick and effective. These days, if my Arrogant Bitch shows up, I just relax and breathe into it. But I seldom experience that energy anymore.

THE LAW OF ATTRACTION

It's a universal law that like energy attracts like energy. So identifying the energy you've been sending out unconsciously, by playing out your stories, themes, and roles, can be a powerful tool for transcending your ego and changing your life.

I remember a client who was desperate to help his son. It seemed the 22-year-old could not hold down a job. Every three or four months the son would get fired, and Dad would respond the same way every time. He would yell, swear, call his son names, and grill him about what he'd done wrong. Obviously, the father was not expressing his concern in a way the son could hear. It sounded only like criticism and none too gentle criticism at that.

Working with the father, I did a short energy piece in which I was shown the father standing on his son's path, blocking his way. In order to continue on the path, which represented his future, the son had to go around his father, which meant leaving the path. I asked the father to use his imagination and see himself stepping off his son's path. Then I asked him to stand behind his son with his hand on his shoulder. This let the son know that his father would be there for him no matter what but that he trusted him to make his own choices—that he would back him in his choices and catch him if he fell. I also gave him a mantra and a visualization to use on his own.

The father called me a week later, very excited. His son had been fired from yet another job, but this time the father's automatic reaction was completely different. When his son delivered the news, the only thing that fell out of the father's mouth was, "Do you want a beer?" So they grabbed a beer and sat down on the steps together. The son was in such shock at his father's new response that he started to cry, and then he poured out his heart. He talked about his parents' divorce a decade earlier and other painful feelings he had never shared. His dad had no desire to justify or defend his actions as he had in the past. He only felt compassion for his child.

The father was calling me to thank me for the work that we'd done together. He couldn't believe how quickly it all turned around. I knew it was because we had identified at a subconscious level the energy that he was putting forth in his conflicts with his son; and, by identifying it, he had broken its hold on him. His angry tirade had shifted to compassionate listening, and this called forth a similar openness in his son. In essence, we revealed his inner bully so he could no longer run this pattern with his son.

A good daily exercise is to keep an eye out for people who seem to have the qualities that you are lacking in your life or who seem to be receiving the rewards that you feel you deserve but aren't getting. When you "catch" someone exhibiting these qualities—such as being honest or drawing admiration—give him or her an immediate authentic compliment, even if the person is a total stranger. Because like energy attracts like energy, once you acknowledge him or her for exhibiting this quality, you are opening yourself up to receive this energy for yourself. You're creating the energy of admiration (or whatever it is that you feel you are lacking) outside of yourself, so that, like an image in a mirror, it can be reflected back to you—maybe not in that moment, but in time. The law of attraction will see to it.

This exercise can be used for a multitude of qualities, anything from wanting to have more patience to being kinder or being a better listener. By giving someone a genuine compliment about a quality you truly admire and crave, you are awakening the same energy within yourself. You are activating the part of your nature, such as patience, that creates a similarity of form, and the law of attraction is now in play. Over time, this awareness strengthens, and you are able to elicit this quality on your own. You no longer need an external trigger to awaken it.

There's a wonderful story that illustrates this law at work. A dog was very angry but didn't know it. He entered a house filled with mirrors, and all he saw were hundreds of angry dogs looking at him. This filled him with even more rage, and he couldn't wait to get out of there. Next, a very friendly, happy dog went into the house with the mirrors. This dog couldn't believe his eyes, because everywhere he looked he saw a happy dog looking back at him. This made him even happier and more excited. He loved the house so much he didn't want to leave.

All the people in your life are reflecting your feelings or judgments back to you. Change your self-talk and your feelings will change, and your experiences will change in turn. When we interrupt our negative mindset, we are sending a signal to brain and body to respond in a new way rather than the old, automatic way. This opens up space where new thoughts can come in, which gives us an opportunity to reach for something better. This is how we start living our promises—the start of a lifelong journey of uncovering who we really are.

REOPENING TO BLISS

Breaking free of the limits the ego places on us can be difficult for a simple reason—we are hardwired to be selfish. So often our first thoughts are, *What about me? How does this affect me? What's in it for me?* It's in our nature to want more than we have. We want to be the center of attention, to have more comfort or security, to have others think we're brilliant—and the list goes on and on. So how do we break through these wants and desires? How do we interrupt the selfish tendencies that lead us off track? How can we possibly uncover our promises and discover our true gifts when we are worried about how to pay the mortgage, find our soul mate, lose weight, or land that dream job? How can we tap back into our true essence, the essence of the Creator, that unmistakable pure energy of love?

I believe that if we were allowed to think this was possible, we would all succumb to another innate desire within us: to become and know ourselves to be like God, to share unconditionally without fear of loss or any thought of our own selfish desires. Why? Because what could be more selfish than to be in a state of euphoria, to want that for ourselves and for the world? To embrace the desire to want nothing; to feel complete freedom yet complete connectedness? I had such a moment when I was 24 years old, when I was, I believe, allowed to touch this bliss.

In Chapter 1, I told you a little about what happened when my first brother, David, died—how I dreamed of his death and then it happened just as I had dreamed. Back at home in Florida after his funeral, living in a new, empty apartment, I was a wreck—filled with sadness and self-hatred, completely confused and utterly alone. Longing for clarity and solace, I sat down on the floor in my bare living room and opened the Bible at random. Whatever passage I turned to, those would be the words I needed.

I don't even remember what the passage was about. But at some point while reading, I felt as if something was pulling on the top of my head. I felt the crown of my head being unscrewed, and then a flood of warmth came down into my body, filling me with an indescribable sense of peace and love that resonated throughout my being.

I don't remember how long the experience lasted. All I know is that when I "came to," I opened my eyes and, to my surprise, saw the ceiling. My neck was bent backward, forcing my face to turn up to what I could only imagine to be heaven. When I looked down at my body, I saw that my shirt was completely soaked—from tears or sweat, I wasn't certain which.

The real surprise came when I saw my hands. The rosary I'd been holding had fallen out of my hand and was lying in the center of the Bible, but my hands were open with my thumb and index finger on each hand touching in a typical Eastern meditation pose. Now, at this stage of my life, I would run in the other direction from anything that didn't resemble Catholicism. I'd never even gone to a yoga class, and the word *meditation* just freaked me out. So I was stunned to see my hands in this position. At the same time, I felt grateful, humbled, and free, and oddly complete.

Later I was to discover that this was a crown chakra experience—a spontaneous opening to the pure energy of the Creator. I would learn that it was no common occurrence. And certainly it was a major gift in my life. It allowed me to completely let go of my anger at losing Dave—to get free of that weight on my soul. I do believe that on that day I was touched by the energy of the Creator's unending love for us, which is ours whether we deserve it or not. The ultimate gift you could achieve for yourself through the work we're doing in this book would be to feel this same divine connection.

The greatness we witness when someone is fulfilling a promise and living his or her life's purpose should inspire us to see our own gifts. It should make us want to reveal our talents to the world, rather than diminish us or discourage us or make us feel less than the person we are watching. It's only the ego that gets discouraged or diminished—never our truest, best self.

If you are prone to feeling sorry for yourself because of your life circumstances, then we've reached a pivotal moment. This is where you must either close this book and move on with your life, knowing that you're right—you'll never succeed so you should stop wasting your time—or be willing to say, "Perhaps I was wrong. I'm ready to give up those beliefs that caused me pain." You may never forget something you've suffered—an old story, an old trauma, an old fear—but you can realize the hold it has on you and let it go. If you try it, you may find that it's easier than you thought. The choice is yours.

I'm reminded of the difficulty, uncertainty, and fear I faced in following the path the Creator was showing me, from living the conventional life of a real-estate investor to being a healer. I think especially of one young man who was literally at death's door and his mother's frantic call asking for help. I slipped away from a dinner party to speak with her on the phone, and the information I received was baffling at first. My fear of being wrong kicked in, along with my self-doubt: who did I think I was to have this young man's life in my hands? I had to let those feelings go and trust what I was hearing.

I began to itch over my entire body and my back felt very hot. I was being told that the young man was having an allergic reaction, and the heat led me to focus on his back. "It feels like he's burning up from the inside out," I told his mother. "It's as if there's something screwing in his back. Does that make sense?"

"Yes," she said, to my surprise. She told me he had had titanium screws inserted in his spine during a previous surgery. It turned out he was gravely allergic to the titanium, and his body was shutting down. I was able to help his mother point the doctors in the right direction. Today he's fine and fully recovered from that ordeal.

When I want to quit or it becomes too hard to listen to the obscure and sometimes bizarre messages I receive, I remind myself of the good that comes out of it. I hope you'll have the courage to face your fears as well. You never know whose life you are meant to touch or save.

ᔔTHE PURSUIT OF PROMISESᔖ

Peggy's Third Example

Describe an event that changed the direction of your life.

When I began exploring my skills as a medium, I met a lot of opposition from people around me. My family was concerned (especially my aunt, a Catholic nun), and some friends stopped associating with me because they thought it was the devil's work. The pressure became too great, and I decided to stop practicing mediumship. Immediately, I felt a more evolved channel of communication open—more benign, free of judgment, all-knowing, and wise.

However, several months later, I was awakened in the middle of the night by a booming voice. The voice was stern, and it asked why I thought I had the right to decide what people needed. Hadn't I received healing when I spoke with my deceased brothers? Why would I deny healing to those around me? It was my job to simply help people to heal, not to decide what was good for them!

My tears began to flow as I recognized my own arrogance and fear about other people's judgments. I returned to practicing mediumship, and over time, some of the people who had criticized me apologized and even changed their views. And I made an explicit promise to the Creator: *As long as I'm doing more good than harm, I'll stay on this path, because I will know it comes from you. If that changes, I'm out of here!*

What did you come to desire because of this event?

To stop thinking that I knew what people needed. To no longer let my fear of what other people thought make me act selfishly, and I began to think of others first.

What promise did this experience reveal?

I am Unconditional Love.

Your Third Promise

Describe an event that changed the direction of your life.

What did you come to desire because of this event?

What promise did this experience reveal?

CHAPTER 4

YOUR BODY'S SECRET

*Man has falsely identified himself with
the pseudo-soul or ego. When he transfers his
sense of identity to his true being, the immortal
Soul, he discovers that all pain is unreal. He no
longer can even imagine the state of suffering.*

— PARAMAHANSA YOGANANDA

I'd like to tell you a story that's near and dear to my heart about my niece Kate and her fiancé, Cory. Cory was living his dream as a new Marine going through infantry training in California while Kate stayed behind in Missouri. A few weeks into the training, Cory called Kate heartbroken, afraid that he might have to drop out because he had injured his knee. He was marching 15 to 20 miles a day carrying up to 100 pounds of gear, and he didn't know how much longer he could keep the pain a secret. What Cory didn't tell Kate was that he was also intensely homesick. He missed her, his animals, his way of life. His dream of the Marine Corps was crumbling before his eyes.

Kate called me in Florida to ask if there was anything we could do. She said Cory was so desperate that even though my work made him uncomfortable (all the more so because he was sensitive himself), he was willing to let her make the call. Over the telephone, I did a channeled healing meditation with Kate in which she was directed to envision herself as Cory—to see herself in his body—and then place her hand on her (Cory's) left knee. Note that Cory hadn't told her which knee was in pain.

I was guided to have Kate say a few phrases to the knee—"I'm capable, able, and strong"; "I give myself permission to trust the unknown"—and to allow it to respond. The knee told us how afraid it was to move forward on this path without Kate and how lonely and difficult it was not to have her to talk to. Kate thanked Cory's knee for sharing its pain with her, then visualized beautiful healing light flowing into the knee before she envisioned herself stepping back out of Cory's body. Both Kate and I were able to feel a shift during this process. We couldn't wait to see what, if anything, would happen.

The next morning Kate received a surprise phone call from Cory. Right away he asked her what she had done. He said that during the night he'd had a vivid dream in which a beautiful woman visited him. He thought she might be an angel. He awoke feeling different—calm, self-assured, filled with peace. Then he got out of bed and realized his knee felt perfect, no pain or swelling. He knew instinctively that Kate must have called me and that she had something to do with his dream angel and the instantaneous healing he'd received. He even confirmed that it was his left knee and that the feelings the knee conveyed to us were exactly right.

BODY AND MIND

Kate and Cory were blown away by this transcontinental distance healing, and so was I. However, I wasn't surprised to find that the emotion Cory was feeling but not expressing had come to the surface in the form of physical pain.

Everyone who is dealing with a physical ailment is also dealing with an underlying emotional pain beneath it. Even if we're not consciously aware of the pain, it is there. The physical pain may be old and persistent, or it may be occasional, or it may be new and alarming. Your body is very wise and can hold on to the underlying pain like a secret it keeps from you, just as you would keep a secret from a friend who was not yet ready to hear the truth about his or her situation. Understanding the link between mind and body allows us to learn that truth—to discover the secrets our bodies are keeping and gain access to the painful emotions our psyches are not yet ready to let go of. And uncovering the secrets of the body is not only a powerful tool for restoring our health but also a good way to hone our intuition and reveal our promises. When we identify and release the emotions the body is holding, we free up more of the mental, physical, and spiritual energy we need to connect with our highest self.

I believe that the physical body contains a doorway to the whole universe. And this is not just my belief. Recent research has found evidence of this connection and actually begun to point to the bodily structures where it may reside, such as the hypothalamus, which is the portion of the brain that regulates the autonomic nervous system and maintains the body's systems in their vital balance. Georgetown University research professor Candace Pert, in her book *Molecules of Emotion,* explores in detail how the hypothalamus, which is part of the limbic system, or "emotional brain," acts as a bridge to our inner world—even to the point of identifying specific neurochemicals that may carry emotional messages at the cellular level.[3]

So what does that mean for your mind and your body? How does a feeling such as frustration or fear translate into a condition such as arthritis or irritable bowel syndrome? I like to call the process Simon Says. Your mind is Simon, calling out the instructions—like "Simon says you're an idiot! Simon says this isn't going to work!" If you follow along, you'll go into submission and say, "You're right—I'm an idiot and a failure." Your mind plays this same game repeatedly, so over time an unwanted behavior emerges—something like anxiety that leads to nail-biting. You try to suppress the unwanted behavior and the uncomfortable emotion that accompanies it. As it's pushed down or ignored, the basic emotion can take some disabling new form, like depression, phobia, or rage. And if it's pushed down far enough, it can take up residence in some part of your body. All this is designed to get your attention.

In my energy work, I take the Simon Says process and turn it around. Before you can turn it around, you must embrace, comfort, and acknowledge that emotion or incident by being a friend to the body part, as we've seen. After you have embraced the emotion, the energy dissipates, and you're able to create a new scenario: "Simon says you're happy and in control."

I've worked with many clients whose physical and emotional symptoms cleared up once we uncovered their basis in emotion. They suffered from a variety of issues: physical pain, insomnia, warts, psoriasis, obesity, uterine cysts, phobias. The most dramatic case was that of a young woman who had "incurable" headaches due to a previous brain tumor—her pain went away completely. I'll tell you more of her story a little later in the book. And you can learn how to do this for yourself, just as Kate helped Cory release the fear and pain from his knee.

Only you can determine what is best for you, and how you approach your health concerns is a very personal choice. I feel it's important to follow through with any medical treatment or alternative therapy you may be engaged in, and to seek a second opinion if necessary. But for some people—especially those with undiagnosed ailments—the mind-body method can be profoundly revealing and physically freeing, especially if you can let go of your expectations about the result. What level of miracle you can receive is up to you.

By the way, Cory was able to complete his training without any further physical complications. He went on to many years of service as a Marine, including a tour in Iraq. He is now a police officer, and he and Kate are raising two beautiful sons.

UNLOCKING THE SECRET

Now it's your turn to connect with a secret that your body has been holding for you. We start the process by seeing what parts of the body need attention. What aches and pains, pressures, twinges, or other sensations—such as hot or cold—are trying to reveal themselves?

If it's hard for you to recognize body symptoms, or if you don't feel any right now, I'd like you to use your intuition. Just allow yourself to be led to the first body part that comes to mind. Take a minute, close your eyes, and ask to be shown which body part needs attention, or simply allow your hand to be led to that part, or trust that you will just know which one to communicate with. Believe me, you're not making up the answer, although it may feel that way. Just play along and see what happens. Take a minute now to close your eyes and try this; then write down the body part that came to mind. If there was more than one body part, write them all down in the order they came to you.

Once you have named a body part or parts, the process of discovering its secrets is as simple as talking to your best friend. In fact, you are going to treat this body part just as you would your best friend. You will separate yourself from your body part and listen to what it has to say. I know this may sound crazy to you, but it is important that you try. If you're not willing to try, then you're free to find another way to access this information—or to continue to accept things as they are without the healing that this connection can offer. It's your choice.

If you're still with me, I want you to give this body part as much attention as you would your best friend if he or she wanted to talk over a problem or tell you something important. (If you prefer, you can think of it as if you are a therapist and the body part is your client.) The trickiest part is to get your mind out of the way. One simple technique I use is to address myself by name as if I were really talking to another person. This creates distance between mind and body. I am no longer me relating to myself within myself; instead, I have stepped into the role of best friend or therapist relating to Peggy Rometo.

For example, say the body parts I wrote down were my sciatic nerve and my lower back. If I were doing this exercise and acting like my own best friend, it might go something like this. I might say out loud, "What does my best friend, Peggy Rometo's sciatic nerve, want to say?" I would take a few deep breaths to relax, and then I would record the information that came to me, by writing it, typing it, or speaking it out loud or into a voice recorder. This information would include anything that popped into my head: thoughts, memories, songs, people, and situations are all clues to untangling the underlying emotion. You should always record all the information you get, even if it seems unimportant or unrelated.

Releasing the Pain

Now you're probably wondering what to do with the information you'll receive—how to figure out what your body part is trying to tell you. Well, sometimes you may find that the message comes through loud and clear. Here's an example of how that worked for me.

Several years ago, I had a routine mammogram. The next day I got a phone call saying that the doctors were very concerned about what they saw and that I needed to come back for a second mammogram. As you can imagine, I was shocked and petrified! My three children were ages two, six, and nine at the time. I couldn't imagine having anything life-threatening, and it was scary to think that I might.

I did what I knew to do. I checked in with the guides and asked for information on what was going on and how to heal myself. The answer I received was the process I've just described. So I followed the protocol. I treated myself like my best friend. I asked Peggy Rometo's breasts what they needed to say. And I was shocked at the information that came through and the depth of the emotion I felt as it was being revealed to me.

At the time, I was working full-time as an intuitive, seeing about 20 clients a week, which was taking a toll on me energetically, and I had just finished breastfeeding my daughter. What I discovered was that my breasts were feeling angry and resentful that I had to nurture everyone around me. My breasts told me they were "sick and tired" of being sucked dry and taking care of everyone. I wrote down this information with great surprise. I'd learned to "just do it" at a very early age from my hard-working Midwestern parents. I had had no awareness that I was feeling this resentment in the first place, let alone that it was so embedded in my subconscious—and now in my breasts!

So I let my breasts go on and on, bitching about everything and everyone. My hands were flying across the keyboard trying to keep up with the dialogue. Then I began to feel heat in my face as the complaints mounted about the long hours, dirty diapers, and unkempt beds. Soon I was sobbing from sadness and exhaustion as my mind raged on and on about the injustices of a working mother's life.

Suddenly, those emotions receded as quickly as they had arisen. The thoughts stopped coming, and calmness came over me. Then I was told to visualize white light entering my breasts, filling the space that once held all that anger and resentment. Finally, I was told to repeat this phrase: *I give myself permission to let go. I am fulfilled and happy. I am free!* So I repeated that several times a day while visualizing the white light.

Two days later I went in for the second mammogram. Afterward, I was about to leave when the nurse said the radiologist wanted to see me. When I asked why, she gave me a puzzled look and said she didn't know. The doctor had never asked to talk to a patient before. Normally he just read the scans and passed them on to the next doctor.

As I was led into the radiologist's office, I didn't know whether to be worried or excited. After asking my name, he showed me the form I had filled out listing my profession as Intuitive Healer. Then he asked if I had done something to myself since my last appointment. Startled and concerned, I immediately wanted to know if something was wrong. He said, "On the contrary!" The new mammogram looked perfect—so much so that he thought it was a different patient's scan until my profession caught his eye.

He wanted to know in full detail what I had done. And I gladly told him! While allowing for the possibility that the film used for my original scans had been defective, he acknowledged that something had definitely changed and he was mystified and intrigued by it. But I knew that my conversation with myself and my work to release my anger had made the difference in the mammogram. My emotion was the only thing that had changed.

As you release emotions from your mind, your physical body releases them as well, lifting your symptoms, sometimes momentarily, sometimes forever. This process enables you to get to know yourself a little bit better. It will guide you to intuitively stop using your body as a dumping ground for unexpressed emotions—fear, anger, resentment, anguish, grief—that you might otherwise hold throughout your life (or, if you think in these terms, carry from one lifetime into another). This process helps you reveal your promises, too, because the release of pain frees you to reveal your true essence. The new you will create new life experiences that wouldn't otherwise have been available to you—the fear would have stopped you!

❧ THE PURSUIT OF PROMISES ❧

Peggy's Fourth Example

Describe an event that changed the direction of your life.

After I had a suspicious mammogram, I received healing information from the guides about how to talk to my body and release its emotional and physical pain. This work changed my body at the cellular level: my second mammogram, just days later, was clear, and I was fine.

What did you come to desire because of this event?

To help other people tap into the healing wisdom of the mind-body connection.

What promise did this experience reveal?

I am a Healer.

Your Fourth Promise

Describe an event that changed the direction of your life.

What did you come to desire because of this event?

What promise did this experience reveal?

CHAPTER 5

DEEPENING
YOUR INTUITION

*Expect your every need to be met, expect the
answer to every problem, expect abundance
on every level, expect to grow spiritually.*

— EILEEN CADDY, *THE DAWN OF CHANGE*

We came into this world curious. As babies, most
of us were eager to explore anything and everything,
from our fingers and toes to blades of grass and, if Mom
wasn't looking, maybe even the food in the dog's bowl
or the dirt in the garden.

The intuitive process is a similar process of discovery
through which we learn about ourselves and the things
that interest us in the world. We are already perfectly
wired with the divine spark of consciousness. This connection with the Creator automatically tunes us in to
answers to questions about which we're curious. It's
preset in each and every one of us, just as your body is
preset to breathe. Have you ever wondered something
and then, boom, the answer comes to you seemingly out
of the blue? It happens to me all the time, even with
simple things; for example, I'll be thinking of someone
and then the phone rings and it's him. Remember, as we

saw in Chapter 2, "the blue" is really the Point of Origin, the place of perfect trust and intuitive knowing where all our answers are held.

We use our intuition to make choices on a daily basis, though we may not be aware of it—just like someone who uses her voice to speak, but doesn't yet know that she is an amazing singer, too. My goal is to help you reach a better understanding of your intuitive wiring and learn to use your "voice" in a new way—to access this connection at will for the purpose of revealing your promises and sharing your gifts with the world. In Chapter 2, I led you through one simple practice for accessing the Point of Origin. In this chapter, you'll learn a set of techniques for deepening your connection.

All the work you're doing in this book—revealing each promise, breaking through each old pattern or belief that holds you back, tuning in more and more to your true nature—is accomplished by being present in the moment and trusting your intuition to bring you the information you need. Training yourself to pay attention to the subtle signs of the intuitive flow will help you tremendously in revealing your life's path moment by moment. So we'll start by reading the signs.

YOUR PSYCHIC SENSES

Information comes to us through all our senses, starting with the familiar five—sight, hearing, feeling, taste, and smell—as well as the sixth, or intuitive, sense we all possess. And the five bodily senses have equivalents at the intuitive level—what we might call "psychic senses." For example, think of the word *clairvoyance*: it literally means "clear seeing," and it describes the ability to see things that others can't. Other people's intuitive abilities may use different sensory inputs, such as *clairaudience* (hearing) or *clairsentience* (feeling or gut instinct). Most of us are wired to receive information more readily through one channel than the others.

To get in touch with your innate way of listening to the universe, try this very simple and accurate test: If you were asked to describe someone who had just entered the room, what would you say? Pretend that someone you can picture has just walked in—not someone you know well, such as a friend or family member, but a public figure such as a politician, musician, or actor. Close your eyes and imagine yourself observing him or her. Pay attention to every impression that comes into your mind. When you open your eyes, write down what you experienced in as much detail as you can. Did you see anything? Did you feel anything? Did you taste, smell, or hear anything? Did thoughts run through your mind, and if so, what were the thoughts? Do this before you read on.

To give you an example of this exercise and what it reveals about your sensory orientation, I'll imagine someone whom a lot of people can picture—say, Madonna—walking into a room. Here are some of the sense impressions I get:

Seeing (Clairvoyant):

*As she **walks** into the room, she is **glowing** with a self-confidence that makes her **seem larger** than her **tiny frame**. Her **dyed golden locks, shimmering** with the **reflection of the chandelier,** are **tightly*** *bound at the nape of her neck, giving a severe look to her features. She's dressed in fatigues like a soldier.*

Hearing (Clairaudient):

One of her hit songs, "Like a Prayer," pops into my head as she walks in. I wonder what her voice sounds like in person. I've heard about her humanitarian efforts; people say that in addition to being a star, she really is a lovely person.

Feeling or Instinct (Clairsentience):

I sense, even with the fatigues, a fragility beneath her strong exterior. I would imagine her to be someone who is accustomed to shielding her heart but, once won over, will be fiercely loyal.

Smell (Clairscent) and Taste (Clairgustant):

I'm across the room when she walks in and immediately I begin to smell wild cherries—I have no idea why. It's so powerful that my mouth begins to water, even though there are no cherries in sight. I wonder if it's one of her favorite flavors or maybe she's just snacked on a few.

Now go back to the description you wrote when you did this exercise. Look at the kinds of things you noticed and the way you phrased your impressions. What sense or senses does your description convey? If you're highly visual (clairvoyant), you've probably used a lot of words that describe what you see. You may have literally described the way the person looks, how tall he or she is, the color of her hair and eyes and clothes, whether you find her attractive or not, and so on. If you're more sensitive to hearing (clairaudient), you may have used words that deal with sound—thinking of something this person said, recalling something you'd heard about her, or describing the actual sounds he or she made moving through the room. If you're especially tuned in to feeling and instinct, you may have recorded intangible impressions of her character or situation or relationship to you. You get the idea. You may have more than one psychic sense working at a time—perhaps even all of them at once—or you may have just one, but everyone has at least one.

Now let's say you didn't like the idea of doing this exercise, so you went in the opposite direction and skipped it. You can still get a revealing result. Ask yourself *why* you skipped it. Did you say to yourself, *That **sounds** stupid*? You were using hearing. Did you say, *I don't **see** the point*? You were using sight. Or maybe you thought, *I just don't **feel** like doing this* or *I **am** too busy now* or *I already **know** what senses I use*—all based on feeling or instinct.

In fact, most of the people who skip this exercise will be the ones who "already know," who are operating from their feelings or gut instinct (clairsentience). Another name for someone with this type of intuitive connection is *Divine Knower*. And this is an important point if you're a Knower yourself. Your instincts have already put you in the flow, so while it's true that we all are receiving information from the universe, you actually have a leg up on everyone else. However, you're also the most likely to think you are making it all up. That's why this psychic sense is initially the most difficult to grasp. To get the most out of this book, you will want to continue to play along, to stretch yourself and work on connecting to your intuition through as many other senses as you can. Hang in there! Once you know how to use your knowing, it can be the strongest and deepest sense of all.

THE DIVINE KNOWER

Since embracing my intuitive gift, I have been open to all of the psychic senses: seeing, hearing, smelling, tasting, and feeling and knowing. But my first experience was with clairvoyance and clairaudience. When I was six years old, my grandmother died. Shortly after her funeral, I came out of my room and saw her in the hallway, standing in front of me as clear as if she were still alive. I wasn't afraid; I was actually excited to see her. I could hear her speak to me in my mind. She said, "Hello, Peggy!"

I was so happy that I ran downstairs and announced it to my family. "I just saw Grandma! I just saw Grandma!" Unfortunately, my family assumed it was my overactive imagination conjuring up Grandma because I was missing her. My brothers teased me endlessly about it, and it would be decades before I saw anything with my psychic sight again.

After experiencing my family's disbelief, I must have unconsciously closed down my clairvoyant and clairaudient connection. It didn't matter—the universe simply created a new channel for me. But this channel was a lot scarier. I now began to perceive things using clairsentience—feeling, knowing, and instinct. As a young girl, especially at night, I began to feel things around me. I *knew* something or someone was in my room, I could *sense* it, but I couldn't see it. The presence would often be confirmed by a physical feeling, such as the covers being pulled off me, or something pulling on my feet, or an occasional comforting touch of a soft hand on my face. Keep in mind that I had my own room and slept alone! For years I struggled to feel safe while sleeping. Eventually I managed to suppress those fears with the busyness of life and the rosary my mother had given me to help me fall asleep—until my brother Larry's death, an event so powerful that it reawakened my desire to feel things as I begged the Creator for Larry to come see me to say goodbye.

When I first discovered my gift, in the aftermath of Larry's death, my husband, Bob, was jealous. He had been reading a lot of books on spirituality and searching for his life's path. And then this unexpected ability that I hadn't even been looking for was revealed to me. I found it both frightening and exhilarating. Bob encouraged me to follow this path and helped keep me sane. But toward the end of that first year, after I fully embraced my gift, he started to feel resentful that it wasn't his calling.

One evening we had just gotten in bed and were catching up on some details about his day. I asked him if he had sought help from his guides. He responded rather angrily, "My guides don't talk to me!" Immediately I said a quick prayer in my mind: "Let Bob know you're here!" I started to tell Bob I'd done this, but suddenly he shushed me. "Do you hear that?" He was sitting bolt upright in bed. We both listened as the long blinds in the family room rustled against the wall. Before I could tell him that it wasn't an intruder, he jumped out of bed. He slinked around the corner with his back hugging the wall, slowly working his way out of our bedroom. I kept trying to get his attention, whispering because he'd already shushed me—"Bob! Bob!"—but he kept telling me to be quiet.

At the door, he stuck his head out just enough to see the light switch and flick it on. The sliding glass doors in our family room were open about three feet and the wind was blowing the blinds. We always kept those doors locked to protect our young children from the swimming pool that was only a few steps away. Bob had double-checked the locks on all the doors before getting into bed, so when he saw the doors open, he stepped right back into our bedroom and picked up the phone to call the police.

He still wasn't listening to me, so I tuned in to his guides to find out what was really going on. I saw Bob's grandfather shaking his fist high in the air. "Put the phone down," I said. "We don't need to call the police. I see your grandfather, and he's really mad." Now that he was finally listening, I explained that I'd asked his guides to make their presence known, since he believed they never talked to him.

Of course, we both wanted to know what his grandfather was trying to say after making such a grand entrance! So I asked what message he had for Bob. In my mind I heard him say, "How dare you say we never speak to you!" A minute later, I heard, "*I* opened the family room doors!" Then: "If there was something wrong with your marriage I would have opened the bedroom doors. It's your family history that is causing you pain. You need to begin there!" Bob didn't see or hear his grandfather, but he *knew* exactly what his grandfather's message meant. He began to realize that he was being communicated with, just not in the same way I was. He simply *knew* things.

It would be some time before both Bob and I really gained an understanding about his sixth sense as a Divine Knower. As I sat in our bedroom receiving the information and relaying it out loud to Bob, I was told that he channeled all the time, and he could have gotten the answer himself. I probably looked as puzzled as Bob did. *Bob channels?* Suddenly I got an image of Bob onstage, speaking beautifully and eloquently, as he frequently did in those days as a presenter at real-estate conferences. Of course! He never prepared, *ever,* for a speech. He just stood up and delivered it. In fact, it used to drive his co-presenters crazy that he was never around to "practice."

When I delivered this news to Bob, it was like he was 16 years old and had just been given the keys to a brand-new car. He was so excited and filled with joy—and it made complete sense. He couldn't wait to try it out.

Divine Knowers often don't know how they know things. They tend to be great in business, because their strong and reliable gut instinct allows them to be quick and decisive. However, their weakness is that they can get cocky and self-righteous. That happens when they stop listening to their intuitive knowing and begin listening out of ego, which is most concerned with being right, controlling, or powerful. Here's how you can tell the difference. When you're in touch with your intuitive knowing and saying what needs to be said, everything just hums along. When you say something that comes from ego instead, it will feel "off" to you. You may feel off balance or have a gnawing feeling in your gut. It's the same feeling you get when people tell you they are going to do something and you just know they aren't. Again, you may not know *how* you know—but you know.

TUNING IN

As we've seen, you are already receiving information from other dimensions, and you always have been. I am here to put you in touch with the information that is available to you so you can retrieve the answers to your questions and reveal your promises.

You can tune in to your intuition anytime and any-where, regardless of circumstances; all it takes is focus. In the beginning, it is helpful to have a quiet space to practice, as I suggested in Chapter 2, and a stretch of time in which you know you won't be disturbed. The steps I'll outline below take you deeper into the work you did to access your intuitive knowing in Chapter 2. They'll allow you to get more comfortable asking for and receiving information, and they may help you toward more accurate or nuanced communications.

You can use this process to revisit your Pursuit of Promises questions, going back to your very first turning-point event. Read what you wrote about each event and notice if the way you've described it feels accurate to you. If not, you can intuit a clearer view of the event itself. Then you can ask yourself the second question in the sequence—"What did you come to desire because of this event?"—only this time, instead of relying on your mem-ory, you'll intuit an answer that may feel more complete.

Below, I'll give detailed instructions for the process

of tuning in to your intuition, and I'll also give you a "cheat sheet" that sums up the steps for quick reference. After that, I'll guide you through an energy piece on the Website, called "Waking Up," designed to help you relax and release any anxiety about doing the work on your own. Finally, I'll ask you to go ahead and tune in, either by listening to the "Guided Questioning" meditation at www.peggyrometo.com in which I guide you through a version of the whole process—or by returning to the cheat sheet and guiding yourself through the steps. I offer both options because different people learn in different ways. You can try both and see which works better for you.

Please read the whole process through once before doing the steps. You can decide for yourself whether you need to go through any or all of the steps. You may find yourself gravitating toward a few of the steps or coming up with your own method. You may prefer to simply breathe and go with your gut. Play with it and see what gives you the best results.

Steps to Tuning In

1. Simply let go of your day.

You can step away from the pressures of your day through a process known as clearing. Begin with a simple inhalation and exhalation of breath. When you exhale, push the breath out with some force, and then simply let go and relax.

This will help clear your mind and release any heavy emotions or tension or pain in your body. We do this unconsciously all the time; it comes across as a heavy sigh, usually on its own. For example, you're in the middle of a project when the phone rings and breaks your concentration. Your sigh of annoyance is your body's way to release this stress. Depending on how stressed you feel in the moment, spend about 30 seconds breathing deeply.

2. Take inventory of your physical body.

Getting acquainted with your body through the feeling sense is an important step in being able to receive and read psychic impressions. Notice if you have any pains or other sensations: Do you feel hot, cold, or tired? Do you have a headache or backache? You may want to close your eyes to help you focus. Pay attention to every aspect of the way you feel physically. Make a mental note of anything that does not shift.

You may find that you're feeling some pain that isn't even yours to begin with. Sometimes, when we come in contact with others, we naturally "pick up" their pains, emotional or physical. Once you're aware that a physical sensation is not yours, it is easy to let it go. Simply say to yourself, "That's not mine," and exhale as if you're blowing off the pain.

3. Ground yourself through your breath.

I'll offer you two methods for using your breath to ground and prepare you. The first is more free-form, the second more prescriptive. Use whichever suits you best, or combine them.

Connecting your breath with your heart. Close your eyes and take in a gentle yet deep breath. As you breathe in through your nose, follow your breath through the sinus passages. Then, as you exhale, imagine that your breath drops down into your chest, into your heart. Imagine your breath, now in your heart, flipping a light switch and filling your heart with bright white light. Follow that white light down through the trunk of your body, out the bottom of your feet, and into the center of the earth. See yourself traveling down into the center of the earth encased in this white light. When you arrive at the center of the earth, you may notice a symbol that lets you know where you are. It could be a sign that says *Welcome* or an *X* that marks the spot. If nothing pops up automatically, make up a symbol that lets you know you're at the center of the earth. Then inhale the white light back up into your body, allowing the light to fill all the parts and all the cells of your body, even expanding a little beyond your body. Imagine your entire body cocooned in this white light that's anchored to the center of the earth. Breathe out again.

There is a fine line between imagination and intuition. Using your imagination when you first get started is a great way to help you tap into other dimensions through that colorful world of play. When you use your imagination, you are really accessing your intuitive knowing, even if you feel as though you're making everything up, and exercising your imagination will strengthen your intuitive faculties over time. The more you put into play all of the senses that imagination draws on (*feeling* your body, *seeing* the white light or symbol, *knowing* that you're at the center of the earth), the stronger your psychic senses become.

Grounding through breathing in white light. This breathing technique, often taught in yoga classes, is similar to what's known as the Victory Breath. Envision a tunnel of white light, as big around as your body, coming up from the center of the earth. You'll be drawing this light up with your breath, up the front of your body: from the bottoms of your feet up your legs, pelvis, stomach, chest, throat, and face, all the way to the top of your head, on one inhalation. When you reach the top of your head, hold your breath for a second or two, keeping the breath inside your body with your mouth closed. Then, on the exhalation, push the light down the back of your body using your breath—head, neck, shoulders, arms, back, buttocks, the backs of your legs—and out through the bottoms of your feet back down to the center of the earth. Repeat this cycle three times.

On the in-breath, the tip of your tongue should be touching the inside of your upper front teeth and the roof of your mouth. On the out-breath, drop your tongue to the inside of your lower teeth. To make this simpler, you might just imagine that your breath is like a wind tunnel flowing up from the center of the earth. As the wind blows up through you, it lifts your tongue up to the roof of your mouth. After the wind hits the top of your head, it blows back down and pushes your tongue down in your mouth.

Over time, try to work up to doing this breathing technique with your mouth closed. In the beginning most of us do not have the lung capacity to do so. It's more important that you breathe deeply and relax than worry whether or not you're doing the technique correctly. While repeating this breathing pattern, try to release any remaining tension in your body, along with any expectations for the information you are about to receive.

When you're grounded and centered, you have an awareness of actual heaviness in your lower extremities, as well as a sense of oneness or wholeness. When you feel ungrounded, flighty, or scattered, this heaviness is missing and you have a sense of being off balance instead. If you're already very grounded, you may not notice much of a different sensation in your body when you do this exercise. But you may experience greater clarity in doing it, because you'll be using your senses to bring the breath through each body part, which helps you to be more focused and precise.

4. Separate your spirit from your ego.

Imagine that you are floating in a tunnel of light. Now see an outline in the shape of your body, like one of those chalk outlines you see at crime scenes. This outline represents your ego. Imagine the outline of your ego stepping outside of the tunnel of light while your spirit remains within. You might envision your spirit as a symbol or shape or a flame or a color. Hold both images of yourself in your mind—your spirit floating in the light and your ego outside the light—and know you are ready. As soon as you see your ego step out of the tunnel of light, mentally say *Simply trust* as a cue that you're grounded and ready to receive psychic information.

The purpose of this step is to help you let go of any interference from your mind or your ego's opinions or desires. It allows you to see that you are staying separate from the communication. Early in my psychic practice, when I was really nervous about being able to receive clear information, I found this step helpful. I called my ego "Peggy the Personality" to create another layer of detachment; and when I put my ego out of the tunnel of light, I knew I was ready to go. With "Peggy" outside the tunnel, I was now detached from the outcome of my inquiry. My spirit remained in the tunnel of light to connect with the Point of Origin so my questions might be answered.

I don't use this step anymore; after years of practice, I

just have certainty that I'm in that space. Another mind trick you can use to sidestep your ego's interference is to simply tell yourself that you don't care what the answer is, exhale, and let go. Use whatever works best for you.

5. State your specific question.

It's important to decide ahead of time what questions you want to answer through this intuitive process. You can speak the questions out loud or ask them mentally; either way, it's a good idea to write them down. I phrase my questions in terms of someone's *highest good*. I find that using this phrase to underline my intention improves the clarity and the quality of the responses.

It's also important to be as specific as you can when framing your questions. The more specific the question, the more specific the answer you will receive. Sometimes people ask me why they need to get specific. Since the universe is all-knowing, doesn't it already know what they need answered? I tell them to use the analogy of a computer: yes, it contains all the information you need, but you'll get much more relevant results if you narrow down your inquiry, just as an Internet search works better when you narrow your search terms. For example, don't ask, *Should I quit my job?* Ask, *Is it for my highest good to quit my current job? If so, why? If not, why not? If yes, in what month and what year?* For questions such as these, the month and year are crucial. Early in my career, I routinely had the right month but was off by the year, because I didn't ask specifically.

6. Receive your answer.

Acknowledge any and all information you receive, even if it's a memory that surfaces or something that "pops" into your head, even if you think you're making it up. Write your impressions down, type them, or record yourself as you speak them aloud. Continue to write or speak until it feels as if there is no more information or until the information starts to repeat itself.

The information you get may answer your question in various ways. Let's say you ask, *Am I going to get the promotion, and if so, when?* You might see or hear or sense the word *Yes* or the word *No.* You might get an image that indicates yes or no in a way that makes sense to you: I sometimes see a green light or a red light, or a well that's either empty or overflowing with water, or I feel energy that's either flat or vibrant. Or you might get an image of your child's birthday party and the number 12. What does that mean? Well, it's a celebration, so the answer is yes, you'll get the promotion. In what year will your child be 12, and what month is your child's birthday in? That's when you'll get it.

Once you are in the flow, new questions may pop up. Just continue to ask them as specifically as you can and record your impressions fully. The only rule is to use discernment—to trust the feelings you receive along with the information, especially your physical body's responses. If something doesn't feel good or authentic, let it go and start over with step one.

Tuning-In Cheat Sheet

1. Let go of your day with clearing breath.

2. Take inventory of your physical body,

noticing any pain or other sensations.

3. Ground yourself through your breath,
   either by connecting your breath with your
   heart or using the Victory Breath.

4. Separate your spirit from your ego. Cue
   yourself to receive information with the
   phrase "Simply trust."

5. State your question, making it as specific as
   you can and setting your intention for the
   highest good.

6. Acknowledge and record any and all
   information you receive. Trust your body's
   response. If new questions come up, ask
   them, too.

Now you're ready to try it yourself. Go ahead and listen to the energy piece that will prepare you to tune in.

....   *Waking Up*   ....

Get ready to do the meditation, referring to the instructions in Chapter 2 if you need to. Write down a specific question that you would like answered, then write down what you think the answer will be, emptying yourself of all your expectations and opinions, all your ego's wants and desires. When you're done, tell yourself you don't care what the answer will be—just let go.

When you're ready, listen to the "Waking Up"

meditation at www.peggyrometo.com Afterward, you can go on and listen to the next track, "Guided Questioning," or you can leave the site and go through the steps of asking your question and receiving an answer on your own.

Guided Questioning

When you're ready, listen to the "Guided Questioning" meditation at www.peggyrometo.com. Come back to this page when you're done.

Once you've asked and answered your question through the intuitive process—either by listening to "Guided Questioning" or on your own—write down your question and the intuitive answer you received.

Now you can compare the two answers to your question—the one you wrote down before the exercise and the one you've just received. Was it the same information said in a different way, or was the information more detailed? Just notice. This is a good way to use the journal I suggested in the Introduction. Note the date, your question, and the answers. Then you can see what happens, which answer comes true. If you do this exercise repeatedly, you can keep track of both methods and see which one proves more accurate over time.

☙THE PURSUIT OF PROMISES ❧

Peggy's Fifth Example

Describe an event that changed the direction of your life.

Early in my career, my cousin Julie and I talked on the phone every day over a period of months, practicing tuning in. We used stories that were in the news, such as a well-publicized kidnapping, as test cases to check our results. I would channel information, and Julie would let me know—because she could feel it in her body—when my channeling veered off into someone else's thoughts or what someone wanted to hear. Eventually she taught me to sense this myself, a crucial step in my work. With her help, I learned a breathing process that allowed me to live in my body and receive information through the mind-body connection.

What did you come to desire because of this event?

My desire became to help others learn this process because it was so easy and effective and gave me so much detailed, accurate information.

What promise did this experience reveal?

I am Aware.

Your Fifth Promise

Describe an event that changed the direction of your life.

What did you come to desire because of this event?

What promise did this experience reveal?

CHAPTER 6

REVISING YOUR STORIES AND RELEASING YOUR FEARS

*The most powerful thing you can do (and it is
very powerful) to change the world is to change
your own beliefs about the nature of life, people,
and reality, and begin to act accordingly.*

— SHAKTI GAWAIN, *CREATIVE VISUALIZATION*

I once had a client who always felt unhappy in her home. Whenever she was out of the house, she was happy; but as soon as she stepped through her door, she felt a depression come over her. She began to wonder what the problem was—her husband? Her kids? Why was this happening?

To unravel a situation like this, we need to look inward and listen to what we're saying to ourselves in the moment. I encouraged my client to sit in her car in the driveway for a minute or two after she got home, to notice how she felt then, and to pay particular attention to the moment right before she entered the house. She noticed she was feeling good while she sat in the car and still feel-ing good when she put her hand on the doorknob. Then in her mind, she heard herself say, "I am so sick and tired of being here! I hate this place! Get me out of here!"

She was startled, to put it mildly. She had no idea that this was the verbal cue she'd been giving herself for the last several years. But on reflection, she could see where it had come from. She had lost her job a few years earlier; and, as a result, the family had to downsize to a smaller house. Moving in there meant that she had failed. Now, every time she crossed the threshold, that voice spoke up to remind her of her failure. Though she didn't hear it consciously, she felt it in her body and her emotional state.

Once she caught herself in this self-talk, she could start a new conversation, one that created a new pos-sibility for her. She began by saying to herself before she went into the house, "I'm grateful for this home. It's giving me time to catch my breath and sort things out. It's perfect for me and my family right now." Her mood lifted dramatically, and the whole family began to get along better.

DISCERNING YOUR PATTERNS

In Chapter 3, we saw how old stories about your life—old patterns of self-talk, old thoughts and feelings, old fears—can create barriers that block your connec-tion to your promises. In this chapter, we'll look more closely at the hold these stories have on your life and how creating new thoughts can open up new paths of peace and possibility for you.

Trust your impulses throughout this chapter: they are leading you toward your true gifts and your life's work. These impulses will light you up! You're going to get excited, feel fulfilled—and feel scared. This isn't the same as being bound by a fear from your past. If you're not scared, it's not a big enough dream. Breaking through our fear is part of what we need to do to bring our gifts to the world.

As you do the exercises in this chapter, a new pattern may start to emerge, one that shows what really makes you happy. It may be a recurring dream. It may come from seemingly random encounters, even comments from strangers. In my life, I always pay attention when something comes up more than once. When I hear something new, I file it away; if I hear that same something again, and even a third time, then I know I am supposed to act on it. This is how I became a Reiki master. I had no desire to do so—zilch, none. Didn't even know what a Reiki master was and didn't care. It sounded weird to me. (I still think that's funny—here I was calling myself an intuitive, a decade before the word came into vogue, and I thought "Reiki master" sounded weird!) But over a period of two weeks, three different people asked me if I did Reiki, or if I knew what Reiki was, or if I would be interested in doing Reiki. Finally I said, "I get it!"

That day I was having a massage by a very talented therapist, named Elizabeth. As she worked, I told her about the recent synergistic events involving Reiki. She started to laugh out loud and said, "Do you know I'm a Reiki master, and I have a Reiki I class starting next week that I was going to tell you about?"

That was the beginning of my journey to become a Reiki master. Interestingly, I took Elizabeth's Reiki I class and didn't really notice any different sensations in my work or my body. I did Reiki II six months later and noticed only a slight difference. But I figured I might as well go all the way, since that was obviously what was wanted for me, even though I wasn't seeing the entire picture. Six months after that, I received my Reiki master initiation. During the workshop in which I was initiated, I was working on a person, and suddenly I noticed an incredible sensation I had never felt before. It felt like grace. I couldn't even put it into words—I just started to cry. In that moment, I realized how much of my personal energy I'd been using in my work as an intuitive healer, so much that I was getting sick all the time—laryngitis, bronchitis, pneumonia. Reiki took none of my energy—none of "Peggy"—so my energy remained intact. The benefit to my clients, and to me, was huge. And I wouldn't even have known anything was wrong unless I had spotted the pattern and followed the signs through to the end.

So as you go through this chapter, pay attention to the signs you receive. See if you spot a pattern or if you get the feeling *I've heard this before.* If you don't notice any patterns, ask yourself another question: *Why am I not seeing it? What am I afraid of?* And then watch what comes up.

A NEW STORY LINE

Many times the negative patterns we're caught in are connected to past-life incompletions—issues left unresolved whose emotional effects we're still feeling in the present. Since we are energy and our souls have always existed, they carry the memories and energetic connections of our earlier incarnations. Our mind, body, and spirit reawaken those memories in the form of emotional or physical pain when we are up to the challenge of dealing with them. As I've said before, you don't need to believe in past lives to use the information these emotions offer; the insight they lead you to can help you in your life regardless.

I mentioned earlier in the book that I worked with a young woman who had been diagnosed with a brain tumor that was completely incapacitating. She was 20 years old. She'd had to quit school, she stopped riding her horses, and she couldn't even brush her hair without feeling pain. Her life virtually came to a halt. She had surgery to remove the tumor, and the pain stopped for a few weeks. Then it came back. Her doctors did a second surgery, numbing the nerve endings in the hopes that they were the cause of the pain. That worked for a few weeks, and then the pain returned again. The doctors finally felt that they had done everything possible; they referred her to pain management.

That's when our paths crossed at a convention where both my husband and her boyfriend were working. Meeting me in person gave her the confidence to work with me professionally, and we had our first session over the phone. I was told that this young woman had had three past lives that were interfering with her health in this lifetime. As I've mentioned, I often tell clients to think of past lives as "good stories." In one of the stories, she was a nightclub singer and all the rage. Everyone loved her. Then one day the owner decided to replace her and make her one of the backup singers instead of the main attraction, essentially screwing her out of profits and fame. The other two stories had the same theme—life is not fair. Certainly life is not fair when you're 20 years old and told to live with pain for the rest of your life!

So we set out to revise this story. I told her to envision several screws—actual screws—in the back of her head. Then I asked her to see them getting unscrewed and falling out. As soon as this happened, we changed the story line to one in which she bought out the club owner, took over, and became immensely successful.

At the end of an energy piece, I ask clients to give me a number from 1 to 100—just to tell me the first number that pops up. This girl picked the number 7. In my work, this number represents how effectively the subconscious has taken in the change we've made and how much the energy has shifted. The number 100 means 100 percent, complete success. The number 7 meant that she and I had a lot of work to do. I gave her some energy work to do on her own and a mantra to repeat, and I asked her to keep in touch. When I hung up the phone, I was hopeful, but realistically, I wasn't sure how much help I had been.

So I was pleasantly surprised to receive a letter from her a few months later—and thrilled to hear that within a week after our call she was completely pain-free. She went back and shared her story with her doctors, who didn't know what to say. Her next-door neighbor wanted to know if I had hypnotized her! She kept in touch with me for several years and told me that the pain never returned. She went back to school, and started riding her horses again. She called it a miracle, and it felt like a miracle for me, too, to be part of such a profound shift.

WORKING WITH FEAR

The old stories and patterns that hold us back often show up in the dramatic form of fear—and fear is one of the most daunting blocks we have to overcome. But what would you say if I told you that at any given moment you could erase your fear? You probably wouldn't believe me. You'd say it was impossible! "How can I erase my fear of heights when I'm sweating 30,000 feet above the earth in an airplane?" "How can I erase my fear of public speaking when I'm standing speechless in front of an audience?" The fact is you can, and the size of your fear doesn't matter. Whatever your fears, you can actually take advantage of them by discovering how they control you and how you allow them to persist.

Whenever your body is confronted with fear, its physiology responds in the same way. It's the same energy that is blocking you; the only difference is its consistency and intensity. If you're willing to try an experiment, you can make a list of your fears, then confront each one through meditation (for example, visualizing yourself in an airplane or in front of an audience). If you like, you can use the breath technique you learned in Chapter 2 to do this meditation. Then see what results you feel in your body. Heart palpitations, sweating, nausea, headaches—what does your body do to stop you from facing the fear?

We have been trained to avoid these reactions, trained to think that when the body responds this way it's bad. Not necessarily. When you harness the energy of fear, it is actually preparing you to be open to your life's purpose. When you are able to control your fear and move through it without the physical symptoms, you are mastering the mind-body connection. In this way, fears are simply another measure of how far you've come.

I'm referring to fears that hold us back, not those that protect us. Some fears, such as a child's fear of strangers, are healthy. But for an adult, a fear of strangers could lead to isolation and withdrawal, not a healthy way to live. I'm looking to support you in gauging the appropriateness of your fears and not allowing them to run your life. When you tackle these fears head-on, you'll be able to create breakthroughs in areas of your life that have been dormant or where you've had only small success. You can start by doing the exercise below.

Tackling Your Fears

First, think of a fear you have had since childhood. It might be fear of sleeping alone, fear of sleeping with the lights off, fear of dying, fear of losing a loved one, fear of flying, fear of embarrassment, fear of clowns or spiders or thunder—anything that still makes you feel anxious or keeps you from living a peaceful life. Once you've identified a fear that has been with you since childhood—anything from age 2 to age 17—read on.

Write the fear down. For example: *Fear of humiliation.* Then think of all the times you have actually felt humiliated—all the stories and situations in which the thing you feared actually came to pass. Write these down, too. You can do this for any or all of the childhood fears that are still with you. If you see a theme emerging, that may help you decide where to focus your work now. For example, when I think of times I felt humiliated, I find they're mostly centered around body consciousness—having the wrong clothing and so on. Once you've written down your current fears and the situations in which they've confronted you, I'd like you to choose one fear that you want to break through now.

You are going to *actively engage* in that fear by making one of those situations happen. Yes, you read that right. I want you to face a fear. For instance, if you want to break through your fear of embarrassment, I want you to intentionally embarrass yourself. You can do this any way you like, by doing anything you can think of that will make you feel embarrassed. This can be done quite artfully—for example, by planting yourself in front of the door to a bank and asking strangers who pass by, "Excuse me, where is the bank?" People will look at you like you're crazy and tell you it's right there.

We've all put ourselves in positions like this unknowingly from time to time, but what's the purpose of doing so deliberately? The purpose is to let go of the idea you have of yourself: the idea that you have a certain nature, a certain persona, or a certain level of intelligence. By asking an embarrassing question like the one above, you're asserting to your ego that it is not perfect—that it can make mistakes, get embarrassed, and survive. You can even take this a step further and enlist someone to play out an ego-breaking scenario with you, such as yelling at you in a public place or, if embarrassment is linked to body consciousness for you, loudly calling other people's attention to the fact that you're walking around with unmatched socks. Once you've seen that you can tackle your fear head-on and survive, you will be flooded with relief and excitement and joy, because you know you're breaking free of what has stopped you in the past—and now the possibilities are endless.

Breaking Free for Real

You can use this same technique to tackle your fear of a real situation you're facing. For example, if you're avoiding a coworker because you're afraid of what you think he is going to say to you, you can play out the encounter in your mind first and confront the worst-case scenario. Let your body tense and your heart race; see the anger in his eyes, and hear the angry words being spoken. Feel the humiliation, shame, sadness, or your own anger in response—whatever this scene brings up for you. Make it as vivid as you can. The stronger you make the visualization, the more likely you are to succeed in breaking the pattern of fear.

Now visualize the scene shifting. See your coworker changing his mind and apologizing, even laughing. Visualize the whole scene over again, but see yourself handling the situation and your feelings perfectly: asking permission to speak with him for a few minutes, setting the right time and tone, trusting that you have in you everything you need to make it happen beautifully. Feel the shame or sadness drain right out of you through the bottoms of your feet.

Then switch the scene back again to the angry confrontation, only this time observe it differently. Notice that your coworker isn't even talking *to* you, but talking over your shoulder. Realize that he treats everyone like this and there's nothing to be afraid of. Instead, see him as a wounded animal. Listen to his pain. Feel the sense of empathy opening up in your heart. Feel the joy, too, that you can be who you need to be, and this person can respond however he needs to, and it need not affect you anymore. Feel the relief this brings. Embrace it, believe it. You are free!

Now I'd like to guide you on a journey to help you chart your new path. The meditation below will help you open your heart, release your fears, and begin to replace them with ideas that empower you to connect ever more fully with your promises.

················   *Feeling Safe*   ····················

Get ready to do the meditation, referring to the instructions in Chapter 2 if you need to. When you're ready, listen to the "Feeling Safe" meditation at www .peggyrometo.com. Come back to this page when you're done.

Once you have listened to "Feeling Safe," write down what you felt during the meditation—any pictures that came to you, any colors, feelings, memories, phrases, or songs. Any body sensations—hot or cold, tension or relaxation. Write down any ideas that occurred to you, any people or places that came to mind, any flashes of inspiration. You don't have to know what they mean or why they were shown to you. Just write it all down before moving on. This is valuable information about how you process events, and you may refer back to it at some point.

Next, pick a number from 1 to 33. Then turn to the list of Healing Mantras that start on page 163 and find the mantra that corresponds to the number you picked. Saying this phrase over the next few days will help to anchor the energy work you've just done in this meditation. Don't be surprised if you find that the phrase is exactly what you need right now. If it doesn't feel that way, trust that it is and use it anyway.

ℰ⊃THE PURSUIT OF PROMISES℃

Peggy's Sixth Example

Describe an event that changed the direction of your life.

During my first year as a professional intuitive, I had a session with a young woman who had had a brain tumor and still suffered from pain that her doctors could not relieve. I received information about a past life that had left its impression on her, and together we revised its story. That session ultimately freed her from pain and gave her back her life, and it gave me faith in my work.

What did you come to desire because of this event?

To do more of this work and discover more about the process in order to make a difference for people.

What promise did this experience reveal?

I am Trust.

Your Sixth Promise

Describe an event that changed the direction of your life.

What did you come to desire because of this event?

What promise did this experience reveal?

CHAPTER 7

EXCHANGING OLD VOWS FOR NEW PROMISES

If one advances confidently in the direction of
his dreams, and endeavors to live the life which
he has imagined, he will meet with a success
unexpected in common hours. . . . In proportion as
he simplifies his life, the laws of the universe will
appear less complex, and solitude will not be solitude,
nor poverty poverty, nor weakness weakness.

— HENRY DAVID THOREAU

Earlier in this book, I explained what I have come to understand about the makeup of the universe: there are different dimensions to it, and we exist in all the dimensions at once. Our highest self dwells in the highest of these dimensions, where there is no lack, only the pure perfection of the soul. As spiritual beings, then, we are always connected to all the aspects of our souls, but we may not always have access to all of them equally. Some of the aspects may be concealed or blocked, and this causes us to feel a lack in some area of our life or our nature.

Here's a helpful analogy: Imagine that your soul is an elevator. The dimension you are in right now, your physical reality on earth, is the ground floor. The highest floor the elevator goes to is the highest dimension, the utmost perfection your spiritual being can attain. This elevator is built to stop on every floor, but just because it has that capacity doesn't mean that it *does* stop on every floor. There are floors that are blocked off, dimensions that you can't access, places where you don't yet understand which buttons to push to make the doors open. In Chapter 4, we talked about how the physical body has a doorway to the universe; in this elevator, the door to each floor opens through a part of the body. When you tune in to that body part and release the pain it's holding, you can remove the block and open the door.

As we saw in the last chapter, the blocks may take the form of emotional and behavior patterns, old fears, traumas, and phobias, and even past-life events. We've explored how these old patterns and old stories can prevent us from realizing our highest selves. In this chapter, we'll look at one particular, powerful way in which old stories control us: in the form of vows we've made, literally or figuratively, knowingly or unknowingly, that bind us to an old way of being. I'll help you see how an old vow may be influencing your life today and, ultimately, cancel it out so that you're free to reveal your real promises.

HOW VOWS WORK IN YOUR LIFE

A vow is not the same thing as a promise—even in the ordinary sense of the word. Here's how *Webster's New World Dictionary* defines them both:

Promise: A statement binding the person who makes it; ground or basis of expectations; pledge. To make a promise of; to afford reason to expect; to afford expectations.

Vow: A solemn promise; an oath; a promise of fidelity. To promise solemnly, to dedicate as to a divine power.

Both have a tangible presence in the physical world, and both, if broken, have tangible results. If a woman promises to buy your house and then backs out of the deal, she has broken a promise; the result is that you don't sell the property and don't get the money for it. If a man takes vows to enter the priesthood and then leaves it, he is breaking his vows; the result is that he becomes a layperson, no longer wears vestments, and does different work. The same is true of a married couple who choose to break their marriage vows: they leave each other and create separate lives.

The difference is that a vow is a *solemn* promise, distinguished by its weight and by the obligation it implies to something larger than ourselves. It's a sacred covenant between us and the Creator. A vow may grow out of a promise, like a seed bearing fruit—if the energy of its emotion and intention takes root in us—but it has a different effect on our lives. An unkept promise, the everyday kind, is a drain and a drag on us: just think of how oppressed you feel if you've created an expectation, such as promising to call someone or be somewhere, and you aren't living up to it. It slows us down, but it doesn't necessarily stop us. It's like the wind blowing our sails in the wrong direction. A vow we're not living up to, on the other hand, is a complete block. We're not getting anywhere; there's no wind at all.

The Bonds of the Past

When you make a vow, you use your words and your thoughts in combination with an intense feeling, positive or negative. Positive vows can be helpful at the start of a path when we are uncertain of ourselves or need a guide to follow. Wedding vows and religious vows are good analogies here: they offer a template for the life we want to create. They support us in manifesting a desire and give us the energy to keep it alive—as when we vow to loved ones who are dying that we will carry on their work or care for those left behind. They give our spirits a form to grow into.

But all vows can ultimately restrict our nature when they are no longer helping us to fulfill our *real* promises, the life promises you're uncovering as you go through this book. When a vow you've made is not working for you, it can show up as illness or depression, physical or emotional pain, exhaustion or anxiety, or a situation you can't seem to change no matter how consciously you try.

The vow that's holding you back may be one you've taken explicitly in this life: for example, I have had clients come to me in desperation because they've been divorced and are seeking new love but not finding their soul mate. Or they've found a new partner only to realize that they're playing out the same patterns all over again. What's happening is that, while the relationship with a former spouse has shifted here in the physical dimension, in the spiritual dimension, it's as though the marriage vows are still in force.

Or you may have made a vow in a past life—in another story, if you prefer—that is standing between you and one of the life promises you're uncovering as you go through this book. Imagine someone who's discovered the promise "I am Abundance" and is doing all he or she can to embody and fulfill this promise but not getting results—or getting results and then seeing them slip away. Well, let's say that in a past life this person took a vow of poverty in a religious order. And that vow led to such a beautiful and happy and spiritually enriching lifetime for this person that he or she brought it forward into *this* lifetime. The vow of poverty in the past is effectively blocking the arrival of abundance in the present.

CANCELING OLD VOWS

Wherever it originated, such a vow has committed you to a path that is incompatible with something you're trying to embody in your life now. A vow is such powerful energy that the universe keeps waiting for you to fulfill it until you deliberately disavow it. You do this by revising the story through meditation, as we saw in the last chapter, and thereby release the energy that's blocking you.

Take the example of the couple who has been divorced but is still energetically bound by the marriage vow. Even if they can't meet on the physical plane to release each other, one of them can go into meditation to let go of his or her claim on the former spouse and change the outcome of the story to one of compassion, forgiveness, and joy. In the case of the person whose former life under a vow of poverty is blocking abundance in her life today, the story might be reimagined in meditation so that money is no longer seen as an obstacle to spiritual life, but something that can coexist with a spiritual calling without overshadowing it. For example, this person could imagine herself living a successful and abundant life, giving charitably to everyone and still prospering.

Getting to the Source

If a vow that binds you comes from an old story, you'll need to discern what it is before you can revoke it in your current reality. In this case, meditation can help you identify the source of the block, reenact the scene or reimagine the story, and cancel the vow.

One of my clients had a bad relationship with a colleague. This person was constantly gunning for her for no reason that she could see. It was so blatant that other people commented on it as well. During our session, I received information that in a past life he and she had been brother and sister, and when they were young she made a promise that they would always remain close. As she grew older, though, she started to find him suffocating; she wanted to spend time with others, but his jealousy got in the way. So she began to taunt him and humiliate him in front of others, hoping he would leave her alone. At this point, my client stopped me. "People at work have told me that he's jealous and intimidated by me," she confirmed. "Someone said that when he was yelling at me he looked just like a little boy."

We did a meditation together to change the past story line. She visualized herself being kind and genuine to him, and she saw them staying in each other's lives even as they grew up and had families of their own. She saw this harmony begin between the two of them and extend to their families. Then I got information that she should meditate daily for the next few days and send her colleague peace and love. I also received a mantra for her to say: "It's safe to see, I'm free to be me, and all is well."

After our session, she felt much better. She called me a few weeks later to report that her coworker hadn't changed much, but she had. Now he could say anything to her, and it didn't bother her. When he tried to humiliate her, she automatically responded with a smile—not a taunting smile, but a genuine one, as if to say *I'm at peace, and I have compassion for you.* Eventually he lost interest and started picking on someone else.

This is a great example of how it's possible to cancel a vow even when the other party doesn't shift. Because my client had asked for forgiveness in a higher spiritual dimension, she was freed. The broken vow from the old story became her colleague's debt to pay on his own.

Releasing a Broken Vow

If you are isolated from others, stuck in depression, or dealing with an ongoing health issue, you may be working out some past-life issue that has you questioning why you're here. Even if you can identify a trigger for your condition in your present life, such as the death of a loved one or an injury you suffered, the thread may lead back to past incarnations as well, to a vow you did not honor in some much older story.

To whom was the broken vow made? To your best friend? To your sister? To yourself? Whom did you disappoint so greatly that you've lost the will to live? This sense of having failed can burden you with illness, depression, and dread, or it can keep you stuck in a way of life that doesn't come close to your potential. Normally we don't talk about failure or success, but this is your journey, and if you are really feeling stuck, then somewhere in your self-talk you are using these absolutes.

When things are going badly, what is it that you say to yourself? What does your daily self-talk consist of? Do you say to yourself, "I just don't care" or "I wish I were dead" or "I just want to be with my (wife, husband, child, parent) who died"? The seed of that emotion has grown into a negative vow. It's important to go back in meditation to acknowledge and then release this energy that is darkening your life and holding you in place. Trace the feeling ("I don't care," "I wish I were dead") back through this life and lives before it to see where you have let people down, where you have failed, where you have "checked out" because of disappointment or grief. (Remember, it's all right if you feel as if you're making this up—you can still learn from it!) Then use your imagination to see a different story unfolding, one in which you are vibrant, healthy, and happy. In this story you don't need to apologize for anything. Enjoy creating this new vision and draw on all the positive energy you can to make it feel real for you.

A Shift Toward a Miracle

You'll be doing a meditation shortly to help you through the process I've just described, along with some additional energy work to help shift your subconscious toward a new story. But first, I'd like to share another example to show you what kind of shift is possible when you do this work.

I had a client whose life revolved around her family, yet she felt stuck and helpless much of the time. A former Jehovah's Witness, she was just opening up to new avenues of spiritual awareness. She was hesitant to speak with me, but she felt compelled to, though she wasn't sure why.

Immediately I sensed that we needed to do some energy work together that involved canceling a past-life vow. I told her that if she didn't believe in past lives, that was fine; she should just think of whatever we talked about as a good story and focus on the emotions we uncovered. She agreed. Immediately I saw a lifetime in which she was the mother of several young children. One child was sick all the time and had to be hospitalized over and over again. Each time my client went to the hospital to tend to her child, her fear and worry gave her headaches and stomachaches. At this, she blurted out, "Peggy, I get headaches and stomachaches now whenever I set foot in a hospital— so I stopped going. I've even missed my mother's and brother's surgeries!"

It seemed that after that lifetime she had vowed never to set foot in a hospital again. Needless to say, this was causing her great distress. Together, we revised the past-life story, re-creating her trip to the hospital as a happy event. We envisioned her son getting well and coming home with her. At the end, she felt a peace she hadn't had before. I felt that she had successfully released her vow.

Three months later, she called me out of the blue, in tears. She told me that within a week of our conversation her son had been in a terrible car accident. He lay unconscious for 12 hours before anyone found him, and he was airlifted from the scene with a broken neck. It seemed like he might not survive. And my client didn't even have to think about it—she rushed to the hospital and stayed by his side 24/7 without one headache or stomachache. She didn't realize what she was doing until one of her relatives said, "How can you be here? Why aren't you sick?" Then she knew right away what had changed. Her family proclaimed it a miracle, and therefore they expected a miracle for her son as well. And it happened: she told me that he was expected to make a full recovery! In the end, it took a year or two, but he did, even teaching himself to walk again.

The meditation below will help *you* discover vows you have made that no longer support you but are blocking your path in your current life. As you free yourself from the past, you may feel as if you've discovered a miracle drug. Or you may just start to see positive progress in your life. How fast you recover is up to you.

Canceling Vows

Get ready to do the meditation, referring to the instructions in Chapter 2 if you need to. When you're ready, listen to the "Canceling Vows" meditation at www.peggyrometo.com. Come back to this page when you're done.

While you were listening to "Canceling Vows," you should have chosen two numbers—the first from 1 to

9, the second from 1 to 5. Just trust whatever numbers you picked.

The first number identifies a color and its corresponding chakra—one of the energy centers in your body. The second number identifies a mantra that's appropriate for you right now. Write them down, then turn to page 170 to find your numbers in the list of Colors and Chakras and the list of Mantras for Canceling Vows.

Used together, this chakra and mantra will help you anchor the shift you've made in this meditation. Here's how: Using the color and chakra you chose, visualize breathing that color into that part of your body. For example, if you chose the heart chakra (green), breathe in beautiful green light and see it flooding your chest and filling your heart. Then speak your mantra out loud. Do this light work three times a day for three days in a row, if you can. It shouldn't take you more than a minute or two each time.

················ *Additional Light Work* ················

For most people, doing the meditation and the three days of chakra and mantra work will be enough. But if your meditation led you to a specific past life and you would like to change that story in greater detail, you can use this process.

1. Write down any memories that came to the surface or any story line that developed in your mind as you went through the meditation. What do you think its significance is for your life now? Can you see how it's blocking your current life?

2. In your mind, pick up the story you were
    shown right at the point where it gets
    bad, and change it to one in which you
    live happily ever after as if the negative
    scenario never happened at all. If you
    were drowning, see yourself saved; if you
    hurt someone, see yourself being kind and
    loving; if you were sick, see yourself healthy
    and vibrant; if you died alone and broke,
    see yourself prosperous and surrounded
    with love. Breathe and relax as the story
    gets better and better. Make it as real as
    you can.

3. Anchor this work by closing your eyes
    and picking a color. Just relax and trust
    whatever color comes to mind, and if
    nothing comes to mind, use white. Then
    pick a number from 1 to 33, again trusting
    whatever comes to mind. Turn to the list
    of Healing Mantras starting on page 163
    and find the mantra that corresponds to
    that number. Now, for one minute, repeat
    the mantra out loud while breathing in the
    color you chose. Do this three times a day
    for three days in a row.

THE PURSUIT OF PROMISES

Peggy's Seventh Example

Describe an event that changed the direction of your life.

I had a private healing session with David Cunningham, a hands-on healer from England. At the end of the session, David and I sat facing each other about five feet apart, and he started sending me energy for my eyes. I was holding his gaze when my eyesight completely vanished, along with David and the contents of the room. Everything turned into a white cloud of light.

Then I started seeing etheric beings where David had been sitting. He asked me what was going on; he couldn't see anything but white light either, and he felt his body being used. I must have seen a dozen different figures—and I knew they were the guides who gave me information for my healing work. Here are just a few that I saw: an angel with a rod, a doctor with a stethoscope, a yogi sitting on a pillow, a wise old Native American woman, a bearded man in a robe, and a guy I call Bubba, because he looked like a good ole boy truck-driver type. (That explains my swearing in a session sometimes!) Each picture changed after about three seconds, as if I were viewing a slide show, and I saw each one three times. Later I was told that my guides were using David as a mirror for me so I could see who they were without being afraid.

What did you come to desire because of this event?

To listen to the wisdom of the guides and share it with others.

What promise did this experience reveal?

I am the Gift.

Your Seventh Promise

Describe an event that changed the direction of your life.

What did you come to desire because of this event?

What promise did this experience reveal?

CHAPTER 8

~ஓ~

CHARTING
YOUR PATH

*Keep away from people who try to belittle your
ambitions. Small people always do that, but the really
great make you feel that you, too, can become great.*

— MARK TWAIN

If you have been doing the Pursuit of Promises exercises at the end of each chapter, a theme should be starting to emerge. Maybe you haven't noticed it along the
way, but if you go back now and read the seven promises
you've revealed so far, you may see connections between
them, ways that one leads to the next or a certain area
of life that they all relate to. Perhaps you'll notice that
many of your turning-point events involve situations
where you've felt misunderstood or that most of your
promises address the way you relate to other people.
Whatever the specifics of your experience, you'll likely find that each event makes you a bit stronger, more
viable, and more outspoken, and that any quality you
need in order to bring your gifts to the world will start
to come more and more to the forefront. In my case, the
events began with an "aha"—realizing I had this gift—
and then other experiences, like being able to change

my mammogram, reaffirmed what I was discovering. A life path began to emerge: I was here as a healer to help other people. Though you still have two more promises to uncover in your Pursuit of Promises, perhaps now you can start to see where you're going.

What if life *didn't* get better for you after these events? What if you noticed yourself shrinking rather than expanding, feeling beaten down, or not following through? This probably happened because you didn't have the support you needed. Well, now you do.

A little later in this chapter, I'll explain how your path of promises may intersect with the evolution of our whole world, and I'll share some practices you can use to shed different kinds of light on the path. But first, let's talk about how you can deepen your intuitive sense of the direction in which your Pursuit of Promises is leading.

Your Piece of the Puzzle

Have you ever wondered why some people seem born to shine? Whether they're making us laugh, or dazzling us with their talent for performance, or making our heads spin with the force of their intellect, those individuals have a quality that draws us to them—an inner light that reflects their gifts out into the world. They have identified their life's purpose—their piece of the puzzle—and how it fits into a larger picture. It's natural that they rise to the top of their profession, as they have no doubt made promises on the other side to inspire the rest of us to discover and express our own gifts in the world.

For some of these shining stars, it's been a seamless rise to the top, but others have had to struggle. We can learn from their examples, because these struggles can be important steps on our path. Instead of giving in to the urge to take the easy way out, sometimes you'll need to do what seems hardest. Don't run away from confrontation, from setbacks, or from your pain. When you meet your fears head-on and embrace challenges as opportunities, you're awakening a part of your soul that already has the answers.

Someone contracts cancer, someone else has a devastating car accident, someone else loses the person he or she loves most: you may have heard such a life-altering passage referred to as a "dark night of the soul." You cannot have true revelation unless you go through some sort of darkness. The light is concealed within the darkness, just as a seed is concealed in the earth, shrouded in the earth's darkness, where it transmutes itself and springs forth to new life as a tree.

Whatever loss we experience—even something such as a failure in business—we feel it as a sort of death, the death of the life we knew. Like seeds, we crack open in the darkness and start to transform. In this way, we discover and fulfill our promises. Each time we come out of the darkness into the light, we're uncovering another promise.

So often we rely on our reason alone to figure things out—but our life's path is best charted in a different way, by using our intuition and trusting the flow. It's not that logical reasoning is bad; it's just not the ultimate barometer. The meditation I'll guide you through shortly is designed to help you keep from overintellectualizing your search for the theme that links your promises and points to your purpose. Use it to open up to images, words, thoughts, feelings, and memories that can point you in the right direction. The reason why it's better for you to discern this direction through your own intuitive process, rather than listening to me explain more theory, is simply that you learn best by experiencing. It's a little like showing you a bicycle and describing how to ride it versus having you jump on and ride it yourself.

.... *Simply Trust!* ....

Begin by opening your heart. You can do this just by thinking of it: *My heart is open.* Then think about your life and ask yourself what answers you need to give you peace of mind and help you understand what is next for you. What direction should you take? What is the best next step for you? Take a moment to see if your body wants to respond. If a body part tightens up or tries to get your attention with some odd sensation, just let it go with a deep breath. Let go of any irritation or frustration.

Get ready to do the meditation, referring to the instructions in Chapter 2 if you need to. When you are ready, listen to the "Simply Trust!" meditation at www .peggyrometo.com. Come back to this page when you're done.

Now that you've listened to the meditation, take some time to write about your experience. Write what you felt, saw, heard, and sensed throughout your journey. Describe the bridge you crossed, the tree you leaned against, the beings who joined you there, the gifts of goodness they gave you. Write about the blank canvas, too. What do you want to see there? Up to this point you've been gathering evidence from your Pursuit of Promises life experiences to show you that you can not only survive but thrive. Now it's time to start making a shift toward creating your own future. What will you create? Were any clues revealed to you?

UNIVERSAL PROMISES

Our personal promises—the kind you've been revealing in the Pursuit of Promises process throughout this book—are specific to each of us. Even if you discover that one of your promises is *I am Peace,* as I did in my first example, it means something different for you than it does for me, and it represents a step on your individual path in this life. But there's another kind of promise we are engaged in fulfilling, even as we're following our personal paths—one that goes beyond our individual lives to help the whole world along its path to unity. I call these Universal Promises.

Universal Promises are transcendent qualities that all souls have the potential to embody in their lifetimes—higher purposes that better the world, such as the promise to love unconditionally or to enable others' spiritual awakening. These ideas may sound rather abstract, but we don't have to think about our Universal Promises in the abstract or pick them out of the air. We connect with them simply by uncovering and consciously fulfilling our personal promises. For example, if you're working on a personal promise of forgiveness and going about it by actively letting go of anger and making peace with someone close to you, then you are engaging a Universal Promise of forgiveness at the same time.

Universal Promises are promises not just for you but also for the world. Each one that's fulfilled brings the world closer to unity with the Creator, because it energetically affects other people, even those who are living disconnected and mindless lives. If enough of us fulfill our Universal Promises, we will eventually reach a tipping point that brings about an end to chaos and suffering on our planet. Gandhi famously said, "Be the change you want to see in the world"—so act as if *you* are the one person who will tip the scales. By fulfilling your personal promises—in other words, by living your own life and being your best self—you can shift the consciousness of the world and help it on its path to peace.

Look at Mother Teresa of Calcutta: she embodies the Universal Promise of unconditional love, which is, in fact, the ultimate promise that all souls will eventually come to. On the road to this Ultimate Promise, she fulfilled personal promises by meeting hardships in her own life. Her father died when she was 8; she was drawn into religious life with the Sisters of Loreto in 1929 when she was 18 and took her vows two years later. She worked as a teacher, and eventually as principal, at St. Mary's High School in Calcutta until 1944, when she made the most difficult choice about her service. She was diagnosed with tuberculosis and was on her way to the hospital when she answered a call from within, a direct message from God to help the poor.

She chose to do the unthinkable. She resigned immediately from St. Mary's and began working in the slums with those who needed her most. She ignored her personal health problems in favor of comforting others in misery, people who knew no mother and no home, who lived in poverty, filth, and disease. They knew nothing but death, and she chose to educate them about life; she showered them with a mother's love and taught them about God.

Not everyone can live a life of such radical service, and not everyone should. Not all souls are awakened to such a desire to change the world. The point is to uncover the promises that lead you on your own best path. You may not be a Mother Teresa, and that's okay. The world needs you to be you.

Now I'd like to guide you through a meditation to help you focus in on the area of your life where your Universal Promise is operating and open up still more to the information you're receiving.

I Give Myself Permission

As you listen to the meditation, just trust that you will receive the information you need. As images, ideas, sensory impressions, or memories start to come to you, write them down without stopping to analyze, correct, or even read what you've written. This will help you sidestep your logic and your need for control. If you feel confused, write that down, too. Let the information flow. You'll eventually reveal new insights or, at the very least, reaffirm what you know to be true, perhaps with a few added details!

Get ready to do the meditation, referring to the instructions in Chapter 2 if you need to. Set aside about half an hour. When you're ready, listen to the "I Give Myself Permission" meditation at www.peggyrometo .com. Come back to this page when you're done.

If you haven't already done so, write down whatever you saw, heard, and felt while you listened to the meditation. Write as much as you need to without editing yourself or analyzing what you've written.

Wait until you're done: *now* you can read what you wrote and reflect on it. See if you notice a theme emerging. Are your impressions scattered all over the place, or do they relate mostly to a specific area of your life, such as love or work? If you feel confused, try this: close your eyes, breathe out deeply, and say to yourself, "Simply trust." Then open your eyes and let your gaze fall somewhere on the paper with your writing. Trust that whatever you land on is the area where you need to focus first.

Working with Universal Promises

As I've said, you connect with your Universal Promises just by fulfilling your personal promises in your daily life. However, your intuitive process can also give you more direct access to the Universal Promise best suited to help you express your gifts in the world—and, along with it, a clearer sense of your life's path. This isn't meant to take the place of your Pursuit of Promises; rather, it gives you more information about how to follow that path and the area of your life where you need to focus your efforts.

Here's a way to reaffirm or expand on what you've come up with in the work you've done in this chapter so far. Pick a number from 1 to 10. Trust the first number that pops into your mind, even if you feel as if you're making it up. If you get more than one number, use the first.

Now look at the list of Universal Promises that follows and find the Promise that corresponds to the number you picked. Of course there are more than ten Universal

Promises—there may be an infinite number—but I've selected ten for us to work with here.

Universal Promises

1. The Promise to perform miracles

2. The Promise to enjoy life

3. The Promise to heal my pain

4. The Promise to surrender to the unknown

5. The Promise to unite all living things

6. The Promise to love unconditionally

7. The Promise to assist others' spiritual awakening through selfless sharing

8. The Promise to awaken the gifts that have been entrusted to me

9. The Promise to forgive

10. The Promise to enlighten myself for the betterment of humanity

There's one more step to this exercise. Each of the Universal Promises in the list above also corresponds to some aspect of our emotional world—an area where we could be more connected or more fully present than we are. So the *next* list offers ten strategies you can use to focus on a particular area of emotional life and more consciously embody that Universal Promise. I call these Emotional Promises. Using the same number you've just picked, find the item in this list that speaks to your life right now. The "I am" statement at the end of each emotional promise is there to help you implement it.

Emotional Promises

1. To be fearless in the face of adversity; to use integrity and creativity to perform beyond what I have been capable of in the past or what I believe is possible; and to start doing so immediately. *I am safe.*

2. To generate honesty, integrity, enjoyment, and humor; to use my skills to allow others to let go of their immediate concerns; to be carried away with laughter, tenderness, and joy through my willingness to share of my possessions, my worth, and myself. *I am present.*

3. To bring forth powerful and pure changes in the world; to support global economies so that all people may share in wealth, be treated equally, and have freedom of choice by knowing their own worth; to begin this process with myself. *I am fearless.*

4. To support myself and mankind in times of weakness or fear; to embrace my current circumstances. *I am connected.*

5. To create unity among the masses by accepting different cultures, personalities, and choices; to release all judgment; to lead in this endeavor by example. *I am free.*

6. To love unconditionally at all times in all ways. *I am responsible.*

7. To be a behind-the-scenes support system for those who serve in a more visible capacity. *I am valued.*

8. To influence through the use of my voice; to support others in discovering their voices; to teach others how to manifest in the world through discerning their life paths and achieving their goals. *I am grateful.*

9. To be patient; to allow for the growth and development of a physical manifestation of humility, unity, and love by putting aside my own prejudices, fear of failure, or past choices; to trust the unfolding process. *I am pure.*

10. To be curious and open; to use certainty and conviction to let truth unfold; to support mankind in discovering this path of truth. *I am committed.*

For example, if the number 9 popped into your head, you would go to the list of Universal Promises and find *The Promise to forgive.* Then, from the list above, you'd choose "To be patient . . . to trust the unfolding process."

This is the emotional task you need to work through in order to fulfill the Universal Promise of forgiveness.

If you want to connect with your Universal Promise more fully, it's time to get active in your community. Think of one action step that you are going to take to help you fulfill it. For example, if I chose number 8, I might sign up to volunteer with a youth group to help young people understand themselves better. If I chose number 3, I might go serve at a food bank or soup kitchen instead of being angry that I have to start over because I lost my job.

Playing Your Role

For more guidance in fulfilling your Universal Promise, here's a tool to help you identify an area in which to carry out the action step you've just come up with. To start, I'll ask you to pick another number, this time from 1 to 13.

Now look at the following list. You'll see that it offers a different way to look at various life paths: in terms of the practical roles we play in the world. The item that corresponds to the number you picked may not literally represent what you are doing or what you should be doing in your life right now; for example, if you picked the number 3 but you don't work in an arts-related field, you don't need to take it as a sign that you missed your calling or should change careers. In the same way, if you picked the number 4 or 5 but you aren't in either of those age groups, you don't need to say, "Peggy, this exercise doesn't work!" What the life role you pick from this list describes is not your literal circumstances or the reality of a given field, but the energy you are being asked to bring to your work in the world. It describes a context in which you can express your Universal Promise.

In particular, you can use the role you've picked to help you pinpoint an area in which to carry out the action step you decided on above. Someone who came up with 2, Service Industry, might decide to work on his Universal Promise by serving others. Someone who chose 9, World Leader, might decide to seek a leadership role in her community or organization.

Life Roles

1. *Entrepreneur.* People who run the business but are not themselves the assets; the business can run without them.

2. *Service Industry.* Those who are of value to others as part of a larger system of order. (Examples: politicians, physicians, clergy, police, social workers, teachers, nannies, waiters, truck drivers.)

3. *Arts and Entertainment.* The assets-for-hire. (Examples: athletes, actors, directors, writers, inventors, speakers, publicists, media.)

4. *Children and Youth.* Those still attending school or college who don't support themselves financially.

5. *Senior Citizens.* The "wisdom group," those who are no longer employed.

6. *Volunteer.* People who donate their money, time, ideas, or support charitable work, be it once or over a lifetime.

7. *Problem Solver.* Valuable resources to support others who wouldn't be able to overcome challenges without help.

8. *Corporate World.* Those who work cooperatively within a large group of individuals for a greater good.

9. *World Leaders.* The elite whom the masses look to for leadership and guidance; they are held to a higher standard than the norm.

10. *Inspirational or Spiritual Leader.* Those whose main function is to awaken, uplift, and teach others. They lead by example by living authentic, genuine, and caring lives; they are not afraid to stand up for their beliefs and inspire others to personal and public greatness.

11. *Facilitator.* Those who work to create unity, be it between feuding neighbors or hostile nations, and to facilitate change however large or small.

12. *Advocate.* The visionaries and activists who work consciously and passionately to change the structures of our communities— anything from reforming health care to

tackling global climate change—and inspire others to embrace new ways of doing things for the good of the planet.

13. *Humanitarian.* Those who hold humanity in the highest regard of all; the Mother Teresas of the world, whose very survival requires them to give up their livelihoods and even their lives for others' sake. They live on charity themselves and offer charity to others by their selfless actions.

When you put this latest piece of information together with the Universal Promise and Emotional Promise you identified in the first part of the exercise, you may be surprised to find how they resonate with a situation you're in right now. Here's an example. When I did this exercise myself, the number that came to mind in the first part was 7—the Universal Promise to support others' spiritual awakening. The number that came to mind for the Life Roles was 6—the role of the Volunteer. At the time, I was preparing to go on a three-day spiritual retreat, and I had volunteered to help out with setup and administration the day before it started. I had struggled at first with the idea of giving up a whole day in that service, because I had friends in the city where the retreat was being held, and I wanted to see them. So when the results of this exercise indicated that it was right for me to be *volunteering* as part of a *behind-the-scenes support system* to work for *others' spiritual development through selfless acts of sharing,* I felt it affirmed that I'd made the right decision.

It's important to note that when I did this exercise again six months later, both numbers had changed.

Because I had fulfilled those roles and was now working on another project, I received different numbers—
and they were amazingly accurate, too. I hope you'll
enjoy this affirming exercise as much as I did! If it didn't
click for you initially, it may mean you've been resisting
something and this information holds a clue for you.
You need to do this!

ೕ THE PURSUIT OF PROMISES ೕ

Peggy's Eighth Example

Describe an event that changed the direction of your life.

I had learned in meditation that I would begin supporting famous people from behind the scenes. The information specifically mentioned Demi Moore. At that time I did not have any connections with celebrities, even through friends, nor had I ever been to Los Angeles or Idaho, where Demi Moore lived. But without conscious effort on my part, a few short months later she and I were on the phone together. A decade later, our relationship has evolved into one of mutual love and respect, and I consider her one of my closest friends.

What did you come to desire because of this event?

To trust the information I receive and to follow through by letting go. Normally I would have been immensely intimidated to speak with someone of Demi Moore's stature at that stage of my career; but in this case, I was able to remove my fear and my feelings of inadequacy by stepping back and observing my experience from a safe, sacred space of connection with the Creator. This experience, more than any other, gave me the confidence and courage to bring my life's work into the world and to give this same confidence and courage to other people. Thank you, Demi!

What promise did this experience reveal?

I am Safe; I am the Observer.

Your Eighth Promise

Describe an event that changed the direction of your life.

What did you come to desire because of this event?

What promise did this experience reveal?

CHAPTER 9

METAMORPHOSIS

*Rest satisfied with doing well, and
leave others to talk of you as they please.*

— PYTHAGORAS

In the previous chapter, I explained that to fulfill a
promise you must embrace your fears head-on. By facing
and breaking through these fears, you reveal your gifts
to the world. You transform the traumatic events that
are designed to awaken you to your next step, and you
turn that darkness into light.

Throughout this book, you've been learning practical techniques for doing this work—ways to access your
intuition, release the fears and old stories that hold you
back, and reconnect with the Point of Origin. In this
chapter, I'll add to your intuitive toolbox with one more
set of practices to deepen the connection by listening to
your body's wisdom and shifting your subconscious toward beliefs that serve you better. You may be content to
keep using the simpler tools found in Chapters 2 and 5,
or your may already be so tuned in that you don't need
these practices at all. That's fine; it's your choice and
your journey. However, I hope you'll read along to learn
a little more about the metamorphosis that takes place,
around you and within you, when you turn darkness

into light—and to prepare yourself to move forward on your path of promises in the next and last chapter.

There's just one thing I would like to mention before we begin. I believe that sometimes what we want to do and what we are supposed to do are not the same. There's a difference between the adversity we overcome by facing our fears, which is a positive process for moving forward on our path, and the kind of constant blocking that forces us down another path because *that's* the one we're meant to take. So how do you know the difference?

As you face your fears, things continue to move ahead, no matter how afraid you are. Circumstances line up for you, you go with the flow, and it feels literally effortless, because you are transmuting your fear into something greater than you ever expected. When you're fighting your way along a path that is not the right one, there is energy constantly working against you; no matter what you do, the path remains blocked or you're turned in a different direction. When these things happen, I firmly believe you are meant to take a different path. If your original destination is really your destiny, you will reach it another way at another time. Or your new path may lead you to something completely different that gives you the fulfillment and joy you always knew you were meant to have.

THREE STEPS TO TRANSFORMATION

By nature, as human beings, we all have the capacity for abundance. But how do we tap into our abundance when we are feeling shut down by boredom, shame, guilt, anxiety, hatred, or palpable fear? These emotions rob us of life energy. And the more time we spend contemplating the past events that led us to these emotions, the greater the energy drain: if we're focusing on a lost job or a failed relationship, how can we disconnect from the part of the brain that's telling us the sky is falling and get in touch with what is next?

We need to find and clear those blocks of stagnant emotion in our mind, body, and spirit, which, as we've seen, are all connected. By asking specific questions about your fears and where they are located in your physical body, you'll be able to heal physical ailments and at the same time open yourself to new promises and a renewed life purpose. When you treat a body part like your best friend and ask it to confide in you, you can take what you learn—the painful, limiting story—and shift it at a subconscious and cellular level to something new and empowering.

In this chapter I'll guide you through a three-step process of meditations and exercises to bring about your most profound shift yet. First, let's look at what the parts of the process consist of.

Step One: Grounding

You begin this process by grounding or centering yourself. *Grounding* is simply a term for the sensation that's created in your body: relaxed, clearheaded, present, peaceful. Acknowledge the painful emotion quickly and efficiently, without judging it. Always keep in mind that you are right where you need to be, but that doesn't mean you need to stay there.

Grounding begins with your breath, which is a key ingredient in your mental, physical, and spiritual health. Remember the Point of Origin space we explored in detail in Chapter 2: this is where your breath will ultimately take you. You can refer back to Chapter 2 and Chapter 5 for more specific instructions on how to breathe. However, the most important thing is not the technique you are using—it's simply to breathe deeply, evenly, and often!

Step Two: Energy Peace

You've seen the term "energy piece" that I use for guided practices designed to shift the subconscious. Here, I've given this step the heading "Energy Peace" to emphasize the calming effect this practice has on the body. You experience energy pieces much as you do meditations—you drop into a relaxed state of mind by listening and allowing your imagination to go along with the story that's being told. The energy piece works with the subconscious to aid in letting go of beliefs that no longer serve you and replacing them with new, empowering beliefs. You're "scratching the record" of your energy to disrupt those old patterns and in some cases even erase them totally.

In my work, no two client sessions are alike, and I don't expect that any two readers are alike either. For this section, I've requested a meditative energy piece suitable for a wide range of purposes—for anyone who is searching for inspiration, information, or healing. If you are uncertain of your path, it will help restore you to the life you were meant to live, without fear. If you know your path already, it will help lift the fog that keeps you from trusting your footing. Early on, my guides used to tell me, *You provide the trust, and we'll provide the proof.* It worked for me, and I'm sure it will work for you.

Step Three: Anchoring and Light Work

Once we've changed our belief system—scratched the old record—we need to anchor the shift so our new, positive behaviors continue. You'll use mantras for this part of the work, as you've done in other chapters. You'll also do light work designed to dig deeper into your emotions and help you release any unneeded baggage you're carrying.

I do want to mention that not everyone responds to this work in the same way. Some people feel immediate shifts and noticeable changes in their behavior. Others react more slowly, as if the old emotions are being shed in layers over a period of weeks. If you're one of the latter, just make sure that when out of the blue you find yourself feeling angry or weepy, you acknowledge it and release it. Don't try to swallow the emotion, even if you have dealt with this issue more than once. You may be dealing with it at an entirely new level now. Instead, do what I call "bless and release": if you're feeling weepy, walk into a bathroom or some other place where you can be alone, allow yourself to cry hard for two or three minutes, and then stop. If you're experiencing anger, you can punch a pillow or even throw a controlled tantrum: put a washcloth between your teeth, lie down on the bed, and scream and yell and flail your arms and legs. (The washcloth muffles those frightful yells!) Then thank your body for releasing those emotions.

You may have to do this for several days, depending on how deeply your old patterns are rooted. The good news is that you don't even have to know why you are experiencing these feelings. Just be grateful that they have come up to be released, because that means they will no longer hold you back.

SHIFTING YOUR REALITY

Don't underestimate the potential for change in the work you're about to do. Many people have felt immediate shifts and noticed themselves reacting differently in situations that are stressful for them. Those who haven't been able to speak up suddenly find their voices. Relationships suddenly seem better. And all you really need to achieve positive results is to be open and willing, trust yourself, and follow through on what's asked of you.

.... *Just Breathe!* ....

The first step is a short grounding meditation called "Just Breathe!" This is a tool very much like the steps for tuning in that we discussed in Chapter 5. If you like this meditation, you can return to it—either reading it or listening to the music on the Website—anytime you want to as a quick way to get grounded, centered, and calm.

Get ready to do the meditations, referring to "The Meditation Process" on page 22 if you need to. You'll need about half an hour to an hour to work through all three. When you're ready, listen to the "Just Breathe!"meditation at www.peggyrometo.com. Afterward, you can go right on to the "Metamorphosis" meditation.

Metamorphosis

When you're ready, listen to the "Metamorphosis" meditation at www.peggyrometo.com. Come back to this page when you're done.

Write down anything you felt or saw while you listened to "Metamorphosis" that feels important to you. Write any messages you may have received. Take a few minutes to do this now, and then move on when you feel this step is complete.

Anchoring and Light Work

While you listened to "Metamorphosis," I asked you to pick a number from 1 to 5. Trust that your subconscious has picked the right number. Write it down.

Turn to page 190 to the list of Mantras and Colors and find the number you picked. To anchor the shift you've made through your work in this chapter, speak the mantra out loud while you visualize the color associated with it. Imagine breathing the color in and out, allowing it to saturate your entire body, both inside and out, for at least three complete cycles of breath. Do this three times a day for the next three days.

You may be wondering what shade of your color you should use or how to combine two colors if that's what you're given. You don't have to think about this consciously; just trust your imagination and the color as you see it in your mind. The color may even change as you go along—go with it! If you're using two colors, you can imagine them one at a time or see them both at once swirling around you. It doesn't matter.

This exercise should take you only a minute or two each time you do it. That's less than five minutes a day!

If you want to, you can listen to the energy piece again each time you use the mantra, but you don't need to. It's the light work that will anchor the new beliefs in your subconscious.

·············· *Additional Light Work* ··············

The work you've done so far in this chapter is enough to produce a powerful shift! However, if you'd like to take it further, the steps below can help you create even more profound change in your energy and your beliefs.

1. Pretend that you are a journalist and have been asked to write an unbiased article about yourself. Sit down and write out everything that you think people have said or would say about you, good and bad, whether you agree or not. Don't hold back. For simplicity's sake, you could start with the sentence "John is . . ." and complete it over and over again until you run out of things to say. For example: *John is smart. John is helpful. John is angry. John is uncaring. John is caring.* You may come up with contradictions like this, just as in the real world people can have different views of the same thing, depending on their experiences. For example, let's say that someone thinks you're lazy and have lousy work habits. You know this isn't true of you, but that conversation about you is still out there, and it still needs to be written down.

2. Now I want you to accept all that you
    have written down as truth, whether it is
    or not. Acknowledge this by saying the
    following mantra out loud: *I embody all
    communication about me. I willingly accept it
    now.* If you've been the target of malicious
    gossip or involved in a family feud, this
    may be especially difficult. But until you're
    willing to stop being upset and resisting
    what is being said about you, you cannot
    alter the consciousness around you. There's
    an old saying, "What you resist persists."
    Remember, accepting doesn't mean
    agreeing that what has been said about you
    is or ever was true; you are simply accepting
    and embodying it as something that has
    been said.

3. Next, ask yourself where the undesirable
    traits you've written down and accepted—
    true or untrue—are being stored in your
    body. Trust your body and write down
    all the parts that come to mind. Do this
    quickly, without analyzing or editing.
    Simply trust any sensations or body parts
    that come up.

4. Now you're going to take each of those
    body parts individually and ask it to
    talk to you. This may sound silly, but in
    an energetic sense you are *carrying* the
    negative conversation in your body. By first
    acknowledging it, and then listening to it

and thanking it, you can finally release it and the hold it has had on your emotional life. For example, let's say my list reads: *Heart, head, hands, feet, stomach, eyes, liver.* I'll start with my heart, because it's first on my list. I pretend that my heart is no longer part of me; I treat it like a friend, just as in Chapter 4, and I ask it what it wants to say to me. I focus on my heart, breathing light in and out of it for a few seconds, and then begin to write: *Dear Peggy* . . . I continue to write until there's no more to write.

Try this now for yourself. Trust that whatever you write is, on some level, true for you. Allow any emotion you feel—anger, sadness, grief, guilt—to be expressed in the writing. Don't hold back. You may be surprised by what you write!

5. Now you're going to thank the body part that has just talked to you. In my case, it's my heart. So I breathe white light into my heart while I say the mantra I received in the energy piece above. You can use the color light you were assigned above, if you prefer. Trust your instincts! You'll get healing either way.

Measuring the Shift

How can you tell if the work you're doing is working? There's a simple technique I use with my clients to gauge the effects on their subconscious and determine what further work they need. You can do the same thing for yourself when you're sufficiently advanced.

After you've listened to a meditation, pick a number from 1 to 100. The number, which you receive from your subconscious, represents the degree to which your energy and belief systems have shifted in relation to an issue you're working on. When you receive the number 100, it indicates that the new energy is fully integrated in your system. If you receive any number higher than 70, in most cases you can reach 100 in a few days just by continuing to use your mantra to anchor the shift. Once you stay at 100 for two or three days, the shift should stay with you. If you receive a number below 70, it's best to use light work along with your mantra for anchoring.

❧THE PURSUIT OF PROMISES❧

Peggy's Ninth Example

Describe an event that changed the direction of your life.

I co-hosted a local radio show with Cheryl Grace, a feng shui expert. We were broadcasting live from a sports bar when someone asked me to give my pick to win the NCAA football championship. I had a huge fear that I would be wrong—and I was! I picked the wrong team. I received a lot of ribbing for it, and rightly so, because I had let my ego get in the way.

What did you come to desire because of this event?

A second chance to make a public prediction, to redeem myself and support other people in exploring their own ability. To make sure that I have no emotions attached to the outcome of a prediction—no excitement about being right and getting glory, no fear of being wrong and feeling humiliated.

What promise did this experience reveal?

I am Humble.

Your Ninth Promise

Describe an event that changed the direction of your life.

What did you come to desire because of this event?

What promise did this experience reveal?

CHAPTER 10

FULFILLING YOUR PROMISE

What we are is God's gift to us.
What we become is our gift to God.

— ELEANOR POWELL

Our promises in this life are many, and we have a multitude of promises going on at once. Some are brief and concise and completed quickly; others take a lifetime to realize fully. And some, such as the Universal Promise to love unconditionally, may not be completed within a single lifetime at all.

While we've touched on all of these over the course of this book, the big promises you have been uncovering chapter by chapter are the qualities, intentions, and actions you are meant to embody in *your* life, revealed by the turning points on your path and leading up to the current promise that you're working on right now. They are your terms of engagement with the Creator, the guiding principles of the life you're meant to live.

So what does this all add up to? Where does this path ultimately lead?

Throughout the book, you've been looking at significant events to see what effects they have produced in your life—such as my pain after my brother David's death, which caused me to long for peace, or my experience healing the young woman who'd had the brain tumor, which caused me to believe I could heal. In other words, each of your promises has been revealed as an *effect* of some *cause* at work on you. Now you're ready to turn that around. By the end of this chapter, you'll know how to become the cause in your own life and create for yourself the next step on your path.

HELP FOR THE JOURNEY

When you choose to make a promise, the fulfillment of that promise becomes your soul's entire purpose. The soul is endlessly creative in generating ways for you to fulfill your destiny, even if you're not consciously aware of what it's doing, and the universe is endlessly generous in giving you the spiritual support you need, sometimes from what may seem to be the most unlikely sources. I'll tell you a story about one of my clients that I hope may inspire you. It serves as a great example of the support each and every one of us receives to share our gifts with the world.

This client came to me for a phone consultation because she was uncertain about her career path and needed some guidance. She was in the process of opening a restaurant, a complex and costly undertaking, and suddenly found herself questioning whether this was the right direction for her. While we were speaking, she mentioned her deceased father. Immediately I felt another presence come forward and reveal himself as her father. He seemed like a benevolent, wise man, and something about him felt very Eastern. (It turned out that my client was Asian, but I didn't know it because her heritage wasn't reflected in her name or her voice.) Her father gave a beautiful, lyrical description of his ideas and philosophies and how he felt about his daughter. I'm sharing his message to her, just as it came to me in our session, because I feel strongly that it is meant for all of us. I hope you will embrace it as such.

I look at your soul, not at the flesh.

Don't be afraid of life; embrace it and your ancestry and heritage. You are unique, you're a child of the sun, and of your mother, and for that you should never be ashamed.

You will win success through the journey of listening to the wind of your soul. Know that I will always be the one to blow when it is stagnant.

I am at your service and honor you. I will open the door however you wish. It is my privilege to have loved you and to continue on my journey in this manner.

Do not ever feel as if you are disturbing me or as if I have someplace else I would rather be or some other calling; there is none.

You are my gift to the world, my voice will be heard through your voice, my hands will dance with your hands, and my feet will carry you to the best next place. Please allow your heart to listen, to dance, to create, to celebrate the authentic love we share.

Let the moments that you and I give one another be spread throughout the world in lullabies for children who have lost their way. It is for those whose parents have left them, whether through anger, guilt,

shame, drugs, or misguided ways; it does not matter, the children shall not live in shame, for your words will reawaken their souls. I offer this to you, my darling little one.
[He bows.]

"That's my dad?" my client said. "Are you kidding?"

"I would say it's him in his most pure form," I told her. "He showed me petals all around your feet that he's placed there for you, because he feels not even worthy to be at your feet. He's there to serve you. He wants to speak poetry through you. He wants you to write this message, or poem, down, and just as it's healing your heart, he wants you to write songs and lyrics to help heal others. He says, 'You have the gift, wise one—discover it!'"

At this point, my client shared with me that the whole reason she had gone into the restaurant was to create a financial stream that would allow her to do spiritual writing. She took this message as support—totally unexpected but profoundly affirming—to move forward with her plans.

YOUR PLACE IN THE PICTURE

Do you remember the game Telephone? One person would whisper something in your ear and you would listen, then pass along to the next person what you had heard—and so on, with the message taking a slightly different form each time. Information that we receive intuitively is much like this: each of us hears similar ideas, stories, or conversations, but none of us brings them in exactly the same as anyone else. Our impressions are all individual. And each is essential, for within each of us lies a piece of the puzzle that someone else needs in order to reveal his or her own.

If you're reading this book, it's safe to assume that you need to reveal your promises for the sake of the world, to help the world along its path to unity. This is the nirvana we all need to seek. Then you will see no more pain on the planet, no need for control, for there will be only satisfaction. Once mankind has reached this point energetically, when we have all fulfilled our own promises within ourselves and reclaimed our own connection with the Creator, then and only then will this cycle be complete.

Don't be discouraged by my words because you think we are worlds away from achieving this perfection. We are not. The whole planet and all its inhabitants—plants, animals, humans—are awakening at this time, and so are you. Open your arms and your heart to this awareness. Embrace your calling, the gifts that you offer, the treasure that you are. As you do so, you will awaken your brother, your sister, your friends, your neighbors—no one will be a stranger to you anymore.

In 1995, an American family—a couple and their young daughter and son—was crossing the ocean on the adventure of a lifetime: to sail around the world in their 47-foot sailboat. Off the coast of New Zealand, a freighter off course by ten degrees ran them down in the middle of the night and kept on going. The boy was killed instantly; his father and sister clung to the wreckage but soon drowned. In the end, after 44 hours in the water with a broken back and a fractured skull, only the mother survived, haunted almost beyond imagining by what she had endured.

A decade later, a close friend of the family, Hester Rumberg, agreed to help her tell her story. She took two years of her life to do so, living in a basement apartment with no financial support. Even though Hester had no experience as a writer, she knew she was meant to write this. She was compelled to push through her fear and self-doubt (could she do the story justice? could she complete the book at all?) to keep her promise to her friend. Hester self-published the story at the end of 2007 and offered it on Amazon. At once it began selling, and before long agents began calling. Just over a year later, *Ten Degrees of Reckoning* was published in the U.S. and Australia and became an international bestseller.

I know about Hester Rumberg's experience because she is my client. She came to me for validation when she was confronting her fear that she wasn't capable of writing the book, and I helped her confirm that this was indeed a promise she needed to fulfill. Hester kept her promise to tell her friend's story, and because she did, her friend was able to do the same. She survived to honor her family and keep her own promises—to heal her heart, love them forever, and work for maritime safety as a way to keep their memory alive. Ultimately, each woman enabled the other to share her gifts with the world; they could not have done so in the same way without each other. The way you go about embodying your own promises has a direct impact on others' ability to fulfill theirs, so the next time you're hesitating to face your fear and fulfill a promise, ask yourself, *Who else's promise am I breaking?*

Remember, promises are choices we make about where we want to exert our energy. If you're always playing it safe, you can expect to be revealing rather limited and most likely selfish promises. Promises that revolve around you and your wants and needs. Promises that are about convenience rather than courage.

I'd like to share a letter from a client who moved beyond playing it safe and found the courage to face a challenge and fulfill a promise with greater ease and success than she could have imagined.

In December of 2007, I had the great fortune of having a two-hour session with Peggy Rometo. We were introduced through a mutual friend of my husband's, and I was in need of some rather urgent spiritual guidance and support. I am a documentary filmmaker and at the time I was working on a film about an orphanage in Kenya, a project that had been several years in the making.

At the time of our call, 25 of the current 200 orphans were on a choir tour of the United States. The children were slated to appear with musical greats Hugh Masekela and Odette as part of *Songs of the Spirit,* a weeklong tour of artists around New York State. In addition, there was a one-night performance at The Kennedy Center; truly a remarkable journey from heaps of garbage to one of America's most prestigious performing arts centers.

I was having trouble convincing the producer of the tour to give me the contact information for The Kennedy Center. He was keenly aware of the strict guidelines regarding recording events at the Center and discouraged me from pursuing it altogether. I, too, did not want to hamper this great occasion even though I knew it would be fantastic to include in my film. I was feeling conflicted, insecure, and scared.

Peggy spent the beginning of our session centering me and returning me to my purpose and vision for the film. She then told me she would be doing a channeled energy piece and that I should repeat after her. I remember a feeling of calm and trust. The words she spoke seemed to put me in a trancelike state. She told me I was the spokesperson for these children and had been for some time. She told me to stand up for them with confidence, gentleness, and purpose. Then she gave me these words to say before my call:

I honor myself. Be at peace. Be the gift.

I went into a quiet room. Repeated the words she gave me several times and made the call not having any contact information. Every person I spoke with passed me to another without hesitation. Before long I was exactly where I needed to be with permission to film 15 minutes of the show, the same as if I were a prominent news station.

As the film enters the editing stage and the children are home in Kenya, their journey of healing through the arts will soon be shared. Peggy's guidance and mantra carried me through many other stumbling blocks and I rely on it frequently both in my personal and professional lives. I affectionately refer to her as a spiritual rock star. I am forever grateful.

Tracy Christian

Turning Your Promise Around

Each of the promises you've uncovered in the course of this book has been revealed by a significant event in your life. Now you can turn that around: you can use your current promise to actively create the next significant event in your life, a turning point designed to your specifications. This is the final step in the Pursuit of Promises process. It's the point where you go from experiencing the *effects* of things to becoming the *cause*.

As we discussed in Chapter 8, as you've strung your promises together throughout this book, like pearls on a necklace, you may have been able to see how embodying one promise led you to your next turning point. Looking back in this way has helped you discern the connection; now you can use that same connection to look forward and see where your current promise will take you. You can create the sequence of events yourself just by deciding to embody your current promise as fully as you can and setting your sights on an event that you would like it to bring about. It's as simple as reversing the steps in the Pursuit of Promises process. Originally, you answered these questions:

- *Describe an event that changed the direction of your life.*

- *What did you come to desire because of this event?*

- *What promise did this experience reveal?*

Now you'll ask yourself:

- *What promise am I trying to embody?*

- *What do I now desire because of this promise?*

- *What event do I want to bring about, through this desire, to take my life in a new direction?*

Let's say your current promise, revealed in the last chapter, is *I am Patient.* What new desire comes up as you work to embody the promise of patience? What is the best next step in your life that you now can see your way to bring about? Though you've been relying more on intuition than on logic throughout the book so far, this is one place where you can use your logical reasoning to think through and decide on the best course of action. Just don't be too conservative—don't play it safe.

Here's how this works in the example of my own promises, which you've following throughout the book. My last promise, derived from a very public mistake in which I made a sports pick that turned out to be wrong, was *I am Humble.* By embodying the energy of that promise—by standing humbled, letting go of the wish for others' approval and the need to be right—I created a new desire. In my case it was just a variation on the previous: to have a second chance to make a public prediction, this time without attaching any emotion to the outcome, neither humiliation at being wrong nor pride in being right. The turning point I wanted to create was an opportunity to make a public prediction that I would get right, this time in an even larger venue. (No playing it safe!)

Become the Creator

What I've just described is the real metamorphosis, the one that turns you into the creator in your own life. However, before you can begin this process, it's important that you clarify your intention and release any negative emotions around your last turning-point situation. You need to be sure you aren't creating your future out of fear, embarrassment, a desire for security or approval, or any such negative reaction to something you want to avoid.

You were probably setting goals for yourself and your life before you ever picked up this book, and it's likely that those goals arose from some sense of need or lack. Even if you achieve them, such goals, generated by ego and fear, are only temporary. On the other hand, when you set goals that come from your highest self, you are drawing on the energy of the Creator within you, and those goals will pull you toward what you desire instead of pushing away what you fear. This is why the "I am" statement in the Pursuit of Promises process is so powerful: it taps directly into the energy of your highest self, allowing your ego to step aside so you can see the larger picture of the future you want to create, not just for yourself but also for the world.

This is where the energy work you've done in this book is most important. If you haven't yet done the healing piece and related exercises in Chapter 9, it's a good idea to do so now. Then give yourself a week or two to process the information and emotions that have come up. If you still feel pain attached to any of your turning-point events, you can do the exercises again until they are cleared or allow yourself to intuitively pick from any of the other exercises in the book.

When you feel ready to move on, take your ninth Pursuit of Promises exercise and turn it around to take you where you want to go next. You've just gained control of your life—well, as much as anyone can! You are now the creator and you can generate new promises that bring you passion, fulfillment, and joy. You're drawing your life experiences to you now, accelerating your journey toward your life's purpose and creating the life you want to live. And when you make a misstep, you'll know, because you'll get immediate feedback in the form of a mild turning-point event that doesn't work out as you planned.

You know now that what you are meant to be doing in life is exactly what's in front of you, no matter how uncomfortable, unpleasant, or boring it is. Stop resisting it, embrace it, and have fun chasing the fear associated with it. If you want to go in a different direction, create a plan of action but not out of fear or boredom. Look around and see where your interests lie, what you're drawn to. What situations do you want to improve in the world? Where do you see pain in others that you want to replace with joy? Many of us find clues in the areas of life where we have struggled, where overcoming obstacles has ignited our passion. I hope you've also received some useful guidance from the exercises in Chapter 8 that may have illuminated your path and your purpose.

The Long View

The final step in creating your path of promises is to see the bigger picture. Where do you want to be in five years? Think about your goals in every area of your life: career, money, relationships, health. You can use the Pursuit of Promises process, turned around, to create your own five-year plan of passion. Don't be afraid to think big: most of us underestimate what we can do in five years but *overestimate* what we can do in one year, which can cause us to get discouraged early. Remember, your "I am" promises are activating the energy of the Creator within you. Would the Creator think small?

To chart your five-year plan, write down where you want to be in five years. Then ask yourself what point you'll need to reach at the end of each year to get there. Where do you need to be at the end of year four? Year three? Year two? Year one? This may be the opposite of most advice you've heard about setting goals: instead of standing where you are now and struggling to see ahead, you're standing in a place where your potential is fulfilled and looking back to see how you accomplished it.

Break the first year down in the same way, working backward month by month: to be where you want to be on December 31, where do you need to be on November 30? On October 31? Then break the first month down into weeks. You don't need to get any more specific at this point; at the end of each month, you can fill in your weekly goals for the next, and at the end of each year, you can fill in monthly goals for the coming year, adjusting as needed based on what you've accomplished so far. Make the goals as specific and clear, as concrete and attainable as possible—this makes it easy to see if you're staying on track.

At the beginning of each month or week—or even each day if it helps you—I suggest you pick a number from 1 to 72 and work with that mantra from the list of "I am" promises beginning on page 147. As with the light work you've done elsewhere in the book, you can repeat the mantra three times a day, or as often as you like. Use it to tap into the energy of your perfected soul to reach your specific goals.

THE LAST WORD

I hope by now you've come to trust and use your intuition on an ongoing basis and that, through the Pursuit of Promises process, you've revealed a deep and powerful direction to take your life in. You have everything you need to continue what you've begun here and go on revealing your light. My hope is that you will revisit this book every year to ensure that you are creating the life you are meant to live so that your piece of the puzzle falls into place in the world.

I hope you'll welcome each turn on your path, at every stage of your life, and find joy in taking your best next step. I'll leave you with the words of the writer and theologian Carl Bard, who described that step so beautifully: "Though no one can go back and make a brand-new start, anyone can start from now and make a brand-new ending."

❧ THE PURSUIT OF PROMISES ❧

Peggy's Current Promise

Describe an event that changed the direction of your life.

I had a local radio show with Cheryl Grace, a feng shui expert. We were broadcasting live from a sports bar when someone asked me to give my pick to win the NCAA football championship. I had a huge fear that I would be wrong—and I was! I picked the wrong team. I received a lot of ribbing for it, and rightly so, because I had let my ego get in the way.

What did you come to desire because of this event?

For a second chance to make a public prediction, to redeem myself and support other people in exploring their own ability. To make sure that I have no emotions attached to the outcome of a prediction— no excitement about being right and getting glory, no fear of being wrong and feeling humiliated.

What promise did this experience reveal?

I am Humble.

Peggy's Promise Turned Around

What promise am I trying to embody?

I am Humble.

What do I now desire because of this promise?

To support people in awakening to the gifts of intuition and entice them to start exploring their own. To do this by making accurate predictions in large public venues.

What event do I want to bring about, through this desire, to take my life in a new direction?

I want to make an accurate prediction before a large audience in a highly visible venue. (Note: I got my chance when I was asked to predict the results of the finals on the TV show *Britain's Got Talent* in 2009. Susan Boyle, the singer who'd created a sensation in an earlier round, was the favorite, a virtual certainty. It seemed obvious to everyone that she was going to win. I made my prediction on the Website www .wowOwow.com, and then I was asked to appear on Fox News's *Strategy Room* and repeat it. In front of my largest audience yet, I said that Susan would come in *second* but go on to release a record that would go to #1—and I was right on both counts.)

Your Current Promise

Describe an event that changed the direction of your life.

What did you come to desire because of this event?

What promise did this experience reveal?

Your Promise Turned Around

What promise am I trying to embody?

What do I now desire because of this promise?

What event do I want to bring about, through this desire, to take my life in a new direction?

MEDITATIONS, MANTRAS, AND LIGHT WORK

I've included the in the Appendix texts of all the meditations you listened to on the Website so you can read them yourself if that's how you receive information best. You'll also find here some of the lists that I ask you to refer to in various places throughout the book.

These meditations are given here much as they originally flowed to me. They are channeled, so when you hear the word "we," it refers to the guides. The meditations are free-form and not always grammatically correct, because what is most important is the energy that comes through the meditation. That's what allows the shift to occur.

CHAPTER 1

I Am Promises

1. I am Peace
2. I am Connected
3. I am Unconditional Love

4. I am Aware
5. I am Beauty
6. I am the Gift
7. I am Trust
8. I am the Observer
9. I am a Healer
10. I am Healed
11. I am Healthy, Vibrant, and Alive
12. I am Awake
13. I am Joyful
14. I am Grateful
15. I am Satisfied
16. I am Safe
17. I am Trust
18. I am Strong
19. I am Complete
20. I am Certain
21. I am All-knowing
22. I am Serenity
23. I am Abundant
24. I am Humble
25. I am Free
26. I am Relaxed
27. I am Stable
28. I am Confident
29. I am Talented
30. I am Smart
31. I am Earnest
32. I am Present
33. I am Patient
34. I am Passionate
35. I am Forgiveness
36. I am Welcoming

37. I am Unity
38. I am One
39. I am Family
40. I am Harmony
41. I am Compliant
42. I am Accepting
43. I am Sharing
44. I am Open
45. I am Creative
46. I am Exuberance
47. I am Centered
48. I am Respect
49. I am Reverent
50. I am Valued
51. I am Perfection
52. I am Fearless
53. I am Adventure
54. I am Revived
55. I am Nature
56. I am Honest
57. I am Real
58. I am Unique
59. I am Wisdom
60. I am Calm
61. I am Mother
62. I am Father
63. I am Play
64. I am Profound
65. I am Gentle
66. I am Compassionate
67. I am Renewed
68. I am Sustenance
69. I am Life

70. I am Resurrection
71. I am Magic
72. I am Whole

CHAPTER 2

Suitcase Meditation

Close your eyes and imagine yourself going back in time—to a time before you were born, to a time that you find peaceful, romantic, soulful, loving, gentle, beautiful, inspirational, fulfilling, and simply satisfying. And if no time comes into your mind, allow yourself to feel these feelings, relaxing and bringing them into full consciousness as to where you are and where you are going. It's okay if you don't know where you are and where you are going; we're going to help you, we're going to remind you of your life's purpose, we're going to set about to bring in the journey of your lifetime. A gentle nudge in the direction of what it was you wanted to accomplish while you were here on this great planet called earth and what you wanted to do while you were here. What you wanted to improve for yourself, for the world, for mankind. To bring that desire full circle, to allow it to open up and to simply know now how it can come into your body, unannounced, to simply know it, feel it, touch it, to create it effortlessly. To have all the individuals in your life right now around you who can assist you in creating this masterpiece and to not be afraid to ask them for assistance, guidance, funding, and direction or to be willing to move them around a bit so that things may flow better as well. You have all the answers, for you brought them in with you.

Imagine a suitcase that you forgot to open and unpack and that you have had with you all along. See this suitcase appearing before you now. Notice the color of the suitcase; if you don't see it, that's okay. Just name the color because you know it's that color or you want it to be that color—it doesn't matter. (Pink, for example.)

Now we want you to see that there is a combination lock on the suitcase, and it's not been opened. Or you may notice that your suitcase is broken open, possibly even by someone else. Maybe its contents are already scattered about, and you are noticing the presence of fear in your belly. Don't be alarmed, you're safe, you're still in control, it's not too late; your ideas haven't been fully utilized by anyone else, and there is still time to capitalize on what you have to offer. You are flexible, and you have resources that have not yet been tapped that can move you front and center into the limelight of success. Keep believing. Keep trusting your instincts. If you have not yet picked up the contents that have been scattered around, do this now.

It may be time to let go, to see that you've come full circle and have done everything that you can, and that it is now time to free yourself up and to allow others to take the reins or to create something new. Just trust what you are feeling and where you are headed. Feel the sky opening up and the clouds parting, the sun coming down and bathing you in its radiance. The suitcase, still in your hand, feels noticeably heavy. You set the suitcase down on your path of life and you choose to leave it, thinking that you can get to where you want to go faster by leaving these contents behind. You hide it, quietly, someplace in your mind, knowing that when the right moment comes, this magical information will become accessible to you. You realize that, as you are present in this lifetime, now is the time—this moment, this book, and this meditation remind you intuitively that you have the answers. You slow down your breathing, you release the pressure to figure it out, and instead you surrender to the higher power of trust, trusting that your Creator would never let you down. Just as your mother wouldn't send you off to school without your completed homework, the Creator would never send you to the earth without access to all that you need.

Your shoulders relax, your jaw releases, your sinuses clear, you begin to breathe easier. Your chest opens and expands with the new rising and falling of your breath; you discover more room around you. You are no longer afraid of failing; you realize that there is no failure, only information, and what you do with the information is up to you. You slowly begin to sense where in your body resides the part of yourself that you can trust; that you can count on; that will never, ever lie to you; that will never, ever tell you only what you want to hear, like a well-meaning spouse or friend. This is the part of you that is divinely connected to the Creator, the part of yourself that is tucked away, until this very moment, for you to discover. Allow this body part to be shown to you now; you may feel it pulse or throb or your hand may intuitively find itself touching this sacred reservoir within you now. Trust where you are led. You have a direct line back to your birth experience, back up to the heavens and back to the time when you were completely and utterly fulfilled. You ask to be taken back there now. It's easy, it's effortless, and there will be no discomfort, no pain, only an observation of what was and an opportunity to embrace this connection in a way that is safe, complete in gentleness and clear and concise communication. You are not alone. As you move back into this space, do not struggle with the idea of constriction or the feeling of being boxed in; instead, let go, go with it, it's temporary, just like earth. Relax, you're safe, you're going home. Breathe in and exhale, moving yourself back up into the womb, quickly and efficiently back into the Creator's arms as a two-year-old who had lost a mother would. Racing, hopeful, joyful, complete, knowing you are safe and you are loved, that you have everything you need. You are free.

Relax your body and slowly embrace this space of clarity. Continue to observe this inner world.

Slowly come back into your body. Now you're ready to begin to write about your experience. This could be in the form of memories, pictures, words, feelings, or sensations in your body. Trust it and allow it to take shape and form. Do not question it, and do not edit it while you are in the flow; do not try to control it or try to direct it. Simply allow it to come as if you are in a stream and it simply washes over you. You're simply observing your experience now.

CHAPTER 5

Waking Up

During this meditation, I'll ask you to repeat back to me the phrases that begin "I give myself permission . . ." These phrases are designed to relax your mind and body, release tension, fears, anxiety, excitement, anything that keeps you from being present. I will give you time to say the phrase out loud before I continue. This is not hypnosis—at least not that I'm aware of; your free will is still intact! Relax and have some fun!

As you close your eyes and relax your mind, feel how easy it is to trust the unknown, to allow yourself to be led down a familiar path, one you have ventured on so many times before. As this path opens up to a beautiful luminous light, feel how easy it is to walk this path of love. *I give myself permission to open my heart and care.* As you give yourself permission to care about your future, about yourself, about your duties and obligations in the world, see yourself letting things go, no longer allowing yourself to get caught up in the nattering of the mind. *I give myself permission to let go of sadness and grief.* Know that underneath this busyness are sadness and grief, humiliation and rage, disgust and fear.

As you close your eyes and walk into a beautiful cathedral, temple, or mosque, feel yourself in this place of worship now. If your place of worship is the roadside, countryside, beach, pool, or pond, feel yourself there. Feel how easy it is to connect to the love of your Creator. As you allow the Creator's love to fill your heart, feel yourself opening the door to a new reality. *I give myself permission to explore the unknown.* As you allow yourself to explore a deeper conversation, one you are excited and enthusiastic about, one in which you know what to do and how to do it. *I give myself permission to excel beyond belief.* As you open a new door to understanding the way in which you receive information, feel how easy it is for you to see the bloom before it is presented, how easy it is for you to know the answer before it is said, how easy it is for you to hear the authentic voice of love without knowing its name. As you trust your instincts and your safety here in this special sacred space that you alone have created, feel yourself getting in touch with your deepest feeling of love. Going back and recalling and remembering a time with loved ones who are no longer present in your life. Feel their energy around you now—the joy and the reemergence of their souls, the heart connection you once shared, and the relief at knowing it still remains. *I give myself permission to love.* As you give yourself permission to love once again, see yourself forgiving them for leaving you too early or staying too long. Feel yourself letting go of old tired energy that has held you back or kept you down.

As you free yourself up to explore the conversations of the sages, feel yourself connecting with higher spiritual guidance, with those you admire, respect, or implore on a daily basis. Allow your mind to see them blessing this experience for you now. *I give myself permission to feel safe and loved.* As you reconnect with your spiritual roots and create a foundation of love in your physical body, feel the grass beneath your feet; feel the beautiful green blades of grass between your toes. As you dig deeper into the soil, feel the rich black earth coming up to greet you, welcoming you home, back to your physical spirit, back to your knowing, back to your community of love. As you feel the centeredness in your body, the wholesomeness of who you are in this journey of love, feel how easy it is for you to receive divine guidance, inspiration, and answers to your questions or new revelations. Trust you will ask the right question to receive the divine knowledge for your highest evolution possible. Welcome the opportunity to return and discover the source of your inspiration, the commitment of your soul, and the willingness to be led and to lead. You are right where you need to be. Namaste, that is all.

Okay. Slowly come back into your body and gently wiggle your toes and stretch whatever and where ever you would like.

Guided Questioning

I want you to put the question in front of you that you want to have answered. This should be on a clean piece of paper without your expected answer on it. Now I'm simply going to walk you through the closed-eyes process of receiving the answer to your question.

Close your eyes. Notice how your body feels; you should feel relaxed. Notice if you are hot or cold or have any aches or pains. Just make a mental note.

Open your eyes and read your question out loud. Read it a few times out loud until you know that you can mentally ask it. If it's too long, you can just say, "Please answer the question I have written down."

Close your eyes again. Just let go of any nervous energy about doing this wrong or doing it right. Just relax and know that you don't need to know how to do this to get results.

Now I want you to imagine that you know where your heart is and put your mind inside your heart now. Imagine that when your mind arrives inside your heart, your heart has to expand to make room for it. Just enjoy the feeling of having your heart expand for a moment or two. Remembering now that you are in control, I want you to take a deeper breath in. Then, as you exhale, the light switch in your heart gets triggered and your heart is flooded with brilliant white light. As you continue to breathe, you are able to expand this light that connects you with the Creator effortlessly.

Follow that white light down through the trunk of your body, out the bottoms of your feet, and into the center of the earth. Become the observer by seeing yourself traveling down into the center of the earth encased in this white light. When you arrive at the center of the earth, you may notice a symbol that lets you know you're there. It could be a written sign that says *Welcome* or an X that marks the spot. If nothing pops up automatically, make up a symbol that lets you know you're at the center of the earth. Then inhale the white light back up through your body, allowing the light to fill all the parts and all the cells of your body, even expanding a little beyond your body. Imagine your entire body cocooned in this white light that's anchored to the center of the earth. Exhale and think the words "Simply trust." Now mentally ask your question again. If it's helpful, imagine now a beautiful white book is placed in your hands. To receive your answer, open the book and watch it unfold.

CHAPTER 6

Feeling Safe

As you let go of duties, obligations, and what you "think" is unique about you, feel your life expanding now. Feel how easy it is to surrender to the unknown. As you stand at the center of the bridge, the bridge that represents both sides of all that is, feel yourself no longer losing control, no longer getting blown by the wind, no longer possessing or wanting what others have. As you determine within your heart chakra now that you have all the lessons, knowledge, and information you need to make clear choices for yourself from this point forward, feel yourself surrendering to what is—whether it is the crushing realization of a life lived uneventfully, or falling off the course of life to discover your addiction of choice, or being raped or raping someone else either in deeds or words, or by conveying secrets. Feel yourself letting go, letting go of the path that you have known that pulls you down, that keeps you tethered to the ground, that makes you feel incomplete. As you slow down now and sit on the bridge for stability, breathe up the beautiful feeling of wood. Feel the warmth of the panels heated by the sun, the slight wearing of the footpaths from the many times you have ventured to do better, you have vowed to quit, you have said, "No more." Release the sadness and guilt of failure or not being the perfect wife, mother, husband, father, brother, sister, child, friend, or parent to another; forgive yourself for not keeping the promises you made to them and to yourself. As you release these inhibitions and no longer second-guess yourself, feel an opening coming toward you. As a magical wind begins to stir, feel the illumination of the sky as the sun begins to shine upon the waters and as the beautiful colors gently glide across the sheet of frozen ice in front of you. You begin to realize that you have been afraid. You have been disconnected. You have shut yourself down, somewhere, some way, sometime long ago on this path that leads to perfection.

You no longer need to be afraid; you only need to be willing to feel. To know deep within your heart what is true for you. What the light wants to create with you as its partner in joy. There is no struggle in this relationship. There is no pain in this relationship. There is only love. Freedom. Peace and tranquility. You must not run away from these feelings, you must embrace them as you know them to be true. They are real. They are you. You have them deep inside of yourself, and they connect directly to the heart of the divine. You do not need to believe in a higher power to feel this connection. You only need to open your heart. You do not need to idolize a saint, a righteous person, an angel, or a friend; you only need to be aware that we are all connected. Just as the water flows from the center of the earth and connects all water systems on the planet, we are connected with one another. You need not pressure yourself to feel concern for others; you only need to open your heart. You may ask how. You may say, "I can't," or you may say, "I won't." It doesn't matter what the mind wants, what the ego wants; we are speaking to you, the soul. The all-knowing part of you that responds automatically, the central nervous system that lights up with excitement because it is being fed. It is being fed universal truths, truths that all mankind needs to hear, that you crave. Your being throbs with excitement, your heart lurches forward, asking for what is next, trying to slow the mind down so that you do not miss a word.

You will not, for the body knows. The body is and will always be in perfect harmony with me, the Light, the presence within you that gives you light. I don't speak through you, I do not tell you what to do. I would never impede your progress in the world. You are the sculptor, I am only the clay. You may mold my essence in any way, shape, or form. You are not the sum of the parts of your being. You are only the conduit from which all life can be felt. You are like the essence of the blossoming cherry; your scent is sensed, then smelled, then seen, then touched and fabricated in your mind.

You are the creator. You are in charge and in control. I am your servant. I am your king. I am all that you want and desire in life. You need not worry or have fear or shame that somehow you are disappointing me, going around me, or blaspheming me. For I am you. To speak to me with such reverence and eloquence is a thing of beauty. I am not disappointed in the choices you have made. I am not angry or ashamed. I am your father, your mother, your friend, and your partner. I am encased in all things you touch. Do not recoil at the thought of offending me; rather recoil at the thought of offending those around you, for I would never abandon you. I would never harm you. I would never treat you with shame, ugliness, or fear. I would not punish you for my own mistakes. I would not beat you for any reason, rape or steal from you for fun or adventure. I would only love. You are I. You have a gift that needs to be expressed and shared. The longer you hang on to the gift the more difficult it becomes to express it and the more obstacles you must overcome to see its lasting vision. And you are at the perfect moment in time to reveal this gift, to allow it to be seen by others, and to listen intently for the signs in the universe to display your gifts to the world. This is the time for revelation—for you to be revealed, unencumbered, unbroken, not dismissive or unkind, and to sink into the knowing now. It may already feel familiar. You may already be on your path. Then why are you on this bridge? What is it your soul is seeking, what depth of emotion has been frozen within you? Arrogance, laziness, entropy? Dissidence, stinginess, insanity, fears? Stubbornness, righteousness, anxiety? What emotional current of disgust are you willing to trade for true peace of mind, for perpetual happiness and joy?

Magically the ice breaks away and the waters are flowing again; large volcanic rocks pop up to the surface. They are buoyant, like you. Feel the heart muscles release and swell, letting go of old negative structures within the cellular mind of your body, no longer allowing you to second-guess where home is. You are here. You are free. You are one with the love of all life. As the water runs clear now and the sun rises overhead, you feel the heat pouring down into your brain. The reassurance you needed to take the next step has arrived, whether it is to end a difficult love affair or not to be in a new relationship that would have you doubt yourself or enlist in a war you do not believe in or fight another man's fight for him. Let go of the struggle, let go of the fear of the unknown. The fear of life itself. The fear of wrong choices. Rather, exhale and embrace peace. The feeling of safety. The knowing that you will be—and are being—guided by the magical life force that you will always be connected to. As this radiance flows down through your head and warms your stomach, feel the calming energy in your heart, the personal sense of satisfaction that you are complete. As your arms tingle with awareness, you may feel weakness. The helpless feeling in the arms comes from lack of faith. You must embrace your knowing. It is your duty. It is your obligation to follow through with your heart's desires, not the ego's desires. The ego's wants are for things to be easy and smooth. The heart's desire is to be free and giving. The two cannot harmonize without free choice. You must face your fears and choose. Do not allow me to choose for you. I cannot. You will only find frustration on the bridge. You must choose for you. You are safe; you have everything you need. You are free.

As the sun slides down behind you, illuminating the soft blue energies of the moon on your back, releasing the pain and shame of loss, of financial disaster, of embarrassment, of loss of youth, friendship, relationship, or family, you let go of the unthinkable. You expand and trust without trying. You breathe in and out with me, your lifeline, the connection with and to all living things. We are all part of this lifeline; you do not need to know how to access it. You just do. No need to complicate the mind-body connection. You must simply make it clear. As if a tuning fork just sounded, the reverberation is felt through the solar plexus, arms, heart, and body. The central column energy is heard—the energy coursing up from the center of the earth, lifting you out of the dormant space that you once thought held everything for you. This raw burst of green energy traveling up through time and space, up through the bottom of your feet, rushing upward exhilarated and excited through the intestines, liver, and pancreas, cleaning out old anger and fear: it is the key to unlocking the solar plexus, the power of your mind, the stomach of your knowing. For it is within this connection that you feel the light energy, the pause that returns you to the Point of Origin, the knowing you are pure. You realize your potential and you step toward it with confidence, full faith, and knowledge that you are being called.

The green energy swirls up further, opening the heart, rushing out butterflies, shooing them away to come back another day. Not today. For today you have no doubt. Today you have no fear. Today you have no trepidation about what is next. You are only willing to believe, feel, see, and know this path as unconditional love. You are free. As the green light flows up through your voice and mind, wonderful, beautiful thoughts begin to emerge. *I am one. I am safe. I am free. I am aware of my divinity. I embrace it now. I expand my awareness. I am a Gift.* You find yourself off the bridge and reconnected to a new path, one you have always known to be true. One you have always felt was right. One that gives you confidence and awareness. You are a sharing being, one who is illuminated so that others may see themselves in you; not one who is boastful, proud, injured, arrogant, or torn, but happy, joyful, and content. As you open your arms you give birth to new enterprise. New fulfillment. New ideas, yet very old ideas. Indeed you are in the flow. A joy swells within your lips, the corners of your mouth smile upward to heaven. Who knew? Who knew it could be so easy to follow your heart? To trust unequivocally that the gifts you have been given are for you—not to keep but to share. To laugh and to spread this joy. To be contagious with life. To let others peek at what you have to offer, and to ask what they are willing to share. The excitement and enjoyment of synergy, of like-mindedness, of joy in community. You have met your match. You are awake. You are ready. You are prepared. Lead now by example, by listening, speaking, and knowing your heart; without excuses, turmoil, or sadness. You are free.

Healing Mantras

1. I accept my life's purpose and myself. I move forward freely and effortlessly with clarity and authentic vision.

2. I'm in love with life. I'm grateful for the unknown. In this moment, I create love, laughter, and freedom.

3. I consciously create a harmonious environment to live, breathe, and celebrate in. I'm free to be me; I'm ready to go. All is well.

4. With confidence, love, and trust I quickly respond to all my needs. I'm free to be.

5. I heal myself with loving thoughts of satisfaction. Thy will be done. All is well. I am at Peace.

6. The environment I create supports me openly and fully to achieve quick and easy results. I appreciate my freedom. Success is mine!

7. I am present to loving thoughts. I invoke satisfaction. I am at peace.

8. I'm satisfied.

9. I move from exile to acceptance of mankind and myself. I am safe.

10. Freedom fills my being. I accept my calling now.

11. I speak confidently with inner strength as my guide. I am at peace.

12. I accept my calling now.

13. With faith, love, and action I excel in life. Peacefully I move forward.

14. I clearly speak my truth. All is well.

15. I trust my choices and myself. I'm free to be me. I honor my past and accept strength from the moment.

16. I trust my abilities and myself. I associate with the unknown freely and effortlessly. I accept my calling now. With love and satisfaction I excel.

17. Confidence lights my way. I am at peace. I clearly speak my truth.

18. I uphold truth, I open the doors to intimacy, and I'm free to be me. I'm ready to go. All is well. Bring it on!

19. With love and jubilation I triumph. It's okay to be perfect!

20. I'm safe, whole, and complete. I'm free to move forward easily and effortlessly. Let us begin!

21. I'm fully satisfied, whole, and complete in my relationships with others and myself.

22. I'm clear about my wants, desires, and wishes. I release anxiousness and accept clarity.

23. I'm true to my word. I move forward fearlessly.

24. Success comes easily for me. I accept my journey.

25. My senses are open and I am awake. I accept my divine knowing.

26. Partnership is easily provided for me. I recognize and accept others in my life. I am worthy of love.

27. Trust comes easily and effortlessly for me. I accept others at their word.

28. Blessings from above renew my health. I am renewed.

29. Abundance flows to me easily and effortlessly. I am safe and secure.

30. I am light and love; together they shine brilliance through my speaking.

31. Creativity abounds. I am rewarded with great enterprise.

32. I trust my ability to heal. I stand whole and complete.

33. I embrace my authentic self. I accept my calling now.

You can use these healing mantras anytime you feel you need added support. Just close your eyes and pick a number—it will always be perfect in the moment.

CHAPTER 7

Canceling Vows

As you close your eyes and open your heart, it's important to know that you're in control. As you give way to new ideas and surrender to the unknown, feel how easy it is to trust. To trust that you have the answers to all of life's questions, that you have already prepared for yourself on this journey the perfect antidote to what ails you. *I give myself permission to succeed.* As you give yourself permission to succeed, see how easy it is for you to go back in time, to remember a place long, long ago where you were uncertain, afraid, destitute, lost, and lonely. You may have been a child who struggled for attention, abandoned or afraid to speak up for yourself; you could have been an adult who persecuted another in a former life. You could have been the henchman who was forced to do heinous crimes. Whatever the sordid story is that holds you back now, allow it to come to the surface. Feel yourself releasing yourself from harm's way, from anger, resentment, poverty, and slavery, sexual or otherwise. See yourself no longer afflicted with pain. As you imagine growing stronger as this weakness is unveiled, feel how easy it is not to judge, not to listen to this old negative programming of not being good enough, of not being able to overcome your circumstances or believing that everyone is against you. As you begin to champion this new stronger voice within you, feel the achiness and pain beginning to subside. Imagine yourself being bathed in beautiful white light. *I give myself permission to breathe.* As you allow yourself now to connect with master teachers from the other side, feel your body opening up to the warmth and magic of healing, the love and surrender that can only be received from the purest of heart.

As you imagine a beautiful baby now being placed in your hands, see the Creator giving you rule over this infant, over its destiny, over its choices. See the white light of the umbilical cord connecting you to the Creator; feel yourself honored to make this commitment and grateful for second chances. *I give myself permission to trust the unknown.* As you look down into this infant's face, you are keenly aware of its familiar lines, the vibration of pure love, of innocence, of hope. As this infant reflects back total awe and surrender to you, feel yourself growing open to new ideas: the idea of being able to start over; the idea of new beginnings; the idea of feeling safe, confident, creative, abundant, and mature. As you allow for this new mind-set to set in, feel the infant lurch in a sudden pain, arching its back up with a memory; calm and centered, you see the problem, you see the memory that this infant has stored for itself so that it would never forget, so that it would never repeat the same wretched mistakes again. You whisper quietly into the infant's ear, "I know. I know. You are a child of the Creator and you are his counterpart. You are free to leave this memory behind. You no longer need it. You are ready to begin a fresh life. You have paid your dues. You no longer need to suffer. Let go now and welcome new beginnings." As you breathe a beautiful blue light into the infant's mouth, you revive it to its present form of purity; you awaken this soul to its destiny. You are freed from the path of loneliness or fear of making the same mistake twice. See the infant exhale old bright red blood, no longer needed to remind itself of the bloodshed from days gone by, no longer needing to remind itself of fear-based conversation. A smile lights up the infant as the light of the Creator shines innocently through its dominion— all the dimensions of the soul and all the restrictions of past incarnations. Magically, all the efforts of all the lifetimes of this child come forward. All the merit this infant has earned and recorded in previous lifetimes is remembered, recalled, and put to use now. Magically this child picks the perfect, time, place, and location on the planet to be born again, the right parents, the right home life, and the right circumstances to embrace. There are no mistakes. There are no redo's. There is no need. You are free.

As the infant wiggles its toe and is born into this lifetime, now feel the inside of your body lighting up with a fresh new hue of light. A new consciousness is brewing and awakened within your solar plexus. Allow your body to ignite this awareness of passion and feel it flooding every cell of your mind and body. Let the mind continue to wander and allow your subconscious to be present, to know what to do and how to do it; to act on its instincts not for pleasure, but for purity. To understand and comprehend what is next for you, for your soul, for this incarnation. As this light grows within you, feel your body taking shape into the man or woman you've become today. Feel the child opening up into new spaces that have been dormant. Feel yourself shedding old incarnations, fears, jealousies, rage, incestuous ideas, murderous revenge, dread, doubt, and death. Fears of victimizing or being the victim, dying of cancer or holding the hand of a loved one in death—no longer seeing this as your future, letting go of all negative seeds that spoil you rotten. Feel the heart awaken now with the beautiful blue-green energy of new beginnings. Above you, the sky is endless and blue; and below, you walk in green pastures of confidence and serenity. And whether you listen now to the Good Shepherd's Prayer and embrace your maker or you allow your consciousness to connect with all that is, it does not matter.[4] For when two souls are joined as one, union is created. Embrace this part of yourself, the awakened one; embrace this jubilant side of you, and know that you are special. You are a child of the Creator and have grown into a magical being, ready to create miracles upon miracles in your life and the lives around you. You are one. You do not need any additional help. You are right where you need to be. You do not need any additional pain to push you in this incarnation now. You are awake. You are alive. You are free. *I know what to do and how to do it.*

Namaste, that is all.

Slowly come back into your body. Now I'm going to ask you to pick a number from 1 to 9. Take the first number that comes to you. Write it down.

Now I want you to pick a second number, this time from 1 to 5, and write it down. Again, take your first choice. You can't get this wrong!

Now return to the book and see what to do with these two numbers!

Colors and Chakras

1. Red—root chakra (genitals)

2. Orange—sexual/creative chakra (pelvis)

3. Yellow—solar plexus chakra (stomach/ digestive system)

4. Green—heart chakra (heart/chest)

5. Blue—throat chakra (throat/neck)

6. Indigo—third-eye chakra (forehead/ between eyes/sinuses/face)

7. Purple—crown chakra (top of head/brain/ thoughts/mental mind)

8. White light—entire body (from the inside out). Breathe white light up from the center of the earth through your entire body and out the top of your head, all the way to heaven. Then imagine when the white light gets to heaven it turns inward and flows back down to you, becoming a soft pink color. Fill your body with this color, all the way to the center of the earth. Used for self-love.

9. White light—entire body (from the outside in). See the white light coming from the horizon toward you and going into your solar plexus. Exhale and imagine the white light splitting: immediately one channel of white light flows up to heaven and the other channel flows down to the center of the earth. Exhale. Used to pull you toward your future and ground you in today.

Mantras for Canceling Vows

1. I am whole and complete. It's safe to see, I'm free to be me. All is well.

2. I know what to do and how to do it. I am free from pain, misunderstanding, sadness, and grief. I am alive, well, and functioning. I am blessed and move forward fearlessly in faith and gratitude.

3. I allow for others to support me. With kindness and compassion I prevail. I move forward fearlessly.

4. I am creative and allow for divine timing. I'm right where I need to be and continue to move forward with passion, reverence, awe, and humility. I am safe.

5. I automatically take the next right step; I clearly see my path as people, places, and things line up to support my destiny. I believe in me. My destiny has arrived. I am free.

CHAPTER 8

Simply Trust

As you close your eyes and open your heart, it's important to know that you're in control. As you give way to new conversation and release old sentiments, anxiety, fear, and trepidation, imagine yourself lying on a beautiful bed of grass. Feel the solid earth beneath you, the warmth of the soil reaching up to embrace you, to reassure you that you are safe, as your desire begins to heat up to be led to the other side to know once and for all your sacred path in life—your ability to heal, to charm those around you, to understand and to clearly know what it is you are being asked to do. Lift up any remaining anxiousness now and hand it off to the Creator to enable you to step forth on this golden path that leads you right to where you need to be. You feel the sun flowing down upon your face; the brilliance illuminates your awareness. You are safe. You are whole. Any remaining fear gives way to the earnest desire welling up in your heart, the desire to remain true to your calling now. As you slowly see yourself sitting up in your mind's eye, rubbing the sleep from it, feeling the cool breeze upon your face, know it's okay. You aren't late; you're here at the perfect time. As relief floods over you that you still have enough time to do what it is necessary in your lifetime, you reach into your pocket and pull out a piece of paper that resembles a ticket. You begin to feel a growing excitement. In your chest an awareness opens up that you are about to travel to a very special place. This ticket gives you permission to access all that you need at this time in your life. You do not need to guess. You do not need to worry. You have everything you need.

Magically a bridge appears before you. As you go now and stand at the foot of the bridge, you notice that the other side of it looks scary. You wonder if the bridge will support you, if you will be able to make it. *I trust my calling now.* As you step upon the bridge with true faith and trust, magically the bridge changes form to a solid path of gold. This golden path swallows up the crevices that were looming so large and deep, where surely death lived. Miraculously the bridge and your fear disappear, and you are still on solid ground. With gold beneath your feet and the wind shifting to your back, feel yourself moving in the right direction. Feel the doors open and hear your name being called. As you allow yourself to be led down this path, you do not need to struggle; there is no fear, only calmness. You smile at how easy it is to allow your mind to relax, to bridge the gap and move forward in the world now. *I open my arms and rest my mind.* As this path gives way to newfound light and stability, see a beautiful tree growing on your path. As this tree magically appears, it is stronger and more brilliant than you could have ever imagined. You are drawn to its trunk, where you gently touch the bark with your hand. You feel the texture as warm and rough—not challenging, but interesting. You also feel something else: a surprise energy of aliveness. You can feel the tree breathing; it invites you to sit and take refuge beneath it. As you lean your back upon this tree of knowledge and miracles, feel how easy it is to breathe with the tree. To feel the flow up from the center of the earth, to not worry about day-to-day living, but rather the emotion of the moment. As you let go even deeper and feel more connected, a branch comes down to awaken you, for you are not alone. A new presence has entered the meadow, and just as a town crier alerts the town to visitors, your awareness is perked. You are listening, you are feeling and sensing that something magical is about to happen. As you release a large sigh of relief and allow a hand to touch your shoulder and to glide down your back, you feel the presence of support—of love, beauty, romance, family union, and divine direction. You are right where you need to be.

As you awaken now to the divinity of being in the Garden of Eden, of being transported to the birthplace of mankind, you feel the benevolent love of all the beings in this sacred place. From the magical colors of the sky to the fields of grain to the dancing hills and the sunlit grass, everything is sacred here. You begin to notice a gathering at hand of teachers, guides, righteous and pure beings of spirit who are here to celebrate your awakening, to prepare you for the journey ahead. As each one steps up to you under this beautiful moonlit sky, you notice there is no time here. Day is night as night is day. You take in the totality of the moment. Everything is here, all the answers of the universe, all your life's work, passion, and play. You relax further into this trusting sense of freedom. You notice a trinket has been placed on your lap. Pick it up and place it in your hand. Feel the connection to this righteous object now and to the devoted master teachers who are here to share with you. They have come to serve you, to inject you with a love that will answer all of your questions, even those you don't know to ask. You let go of the worry of needing to figure it out. You are safe. You are loved. As each of these guides steps up before you and gives you a trinket of goodness that is yours, you continue to relax and feel restored.

Finally, you are asked to understand all that has been given to you. You are asked to convey your true worth and prosperity in the world. Do not be afraid. Be humble, be joyful, and be grateful. The table is set for all to see. Those who come here to serve surround you.

Welcome them. Reassure them that you are here to do your part, you are here to assist, you have a huge thirst in the world to know what you do not know. To see what you do not see, to hear what you have not heard, to taste what you cannot swallow, and to feel what you are afraid to feel. You are gathered in the Creator's arms, nestled safely. A blank canvas is given to you, and you can smell the fabric. You're excited to create and see your dreams. Let go now and trust what is next. Listen with your heart, and allow the message to be conveyed.

You may gently come back into your body and write about your experience, focusing on what is next in your journey of the heart.

I Give Myself Permission

As you close your eyes and trust your instincts, it's important to know that you're in control. As you give way to new ideas and release fantasies that are no longer working or are inappropriate for your life's work, feel your body surrendering to the unknown. Repeat this phrase out loud: "I give myself permission to trust and allow." As you give yourself permission to trust and allow, feel how easy it is to make your mark on the world. How easy it is for you to follow the path that is laid before you. If you let go of self-doubt, fear, and trepidation, you are only left with love. *I give myself permission to love and be loved.*

As you give yourself permission to love yourself and those around you, see yourself no longer holding yourself back for fear of failure. No longer holding back for fear of stupidity or going down the wrong path. *I give myself permission to know what I'm doing.* As you give yourself permission to know what you are doing, where you are to do it, how and when, feel yourself letting go of the why: Why do things need to be so complicated? Why must I do this work? Why can't she just tell me? As you give yourself permission to let go of resistance and of allowing yourself to orchestrate and play in your own game of life, it is important to know that you set up the rules in your life. You create the desire to serve, to accept, to allow, and to turn your intelligence into either stupidity or brilliance. *I give myself permission to take back control.* As you give yourself permission to take back control, feel yourself being led to a new place of business. See yourself no longer second-guessing, no longer wondering what went wrong or how you ended up here. As you allow your body to relax and you feel the earth beneath your feet, feel yourself beginning to understand that you have all the answers within. *I give myself permission to not be afraid; to trust my work, my life, and my circumstances.* As you give way to new ideas of old universal truths, feel how easy it is to allow this information to feel familiar. How easy it is for you to know what to say, how to say it, before it is even said. *I give myself permission to play along, to allow and trust, and to avoid judgment.* As you let go of any heaviness in the chest, any fear of anyone seeing you doing this or of being laughed at or ridiculed, see how easy it is for you to know the score. As you allow yourself to imagine beautiful fields opening up, see children laughing and singing; see yourself walking on the lovely green grass, feeling the solid earth beneath your feet. Notice that everything is in abundance here. There are beautiful mountain ranges, the sky is blue, yet you can see rain coming, just enough to take care of the crops to allow them to bloom in abundance. Notice the animals grazing and the perfect breeze.

I give myself permission to believe. Give yourself permission to believe that there exists outside of our physical world a place that provides sustenance, that all of your dreams and wishes can be fulfilled. That when you touch this place, it feels familiar, it feels like home. It gives you a sense of joy, of belonging; it fills your being with a knowing that we are all connected. *I give myself permission to feel loved.* As you give yourself permission to feel loved, feel yourself letting go of old mind-sets, rejecting logical conversation and dread. *I give myself permission to be wrong about my assumptions.* As you give yourself permission to be wrong about what you cannot see, hear, feel, taste, or know to be known without witnessing, see yourself in a new possibility. *I give myself permission to unveil what I cannot see, what I could not hear, and what I know to be true.* As you give yourself permission to reach this new level of understanding and to come out of this understanding with an ability to love and be loved, feel yourself embracing this sacred day. *I give myself permission to smile and remember.* As you give yourself permission to smile and remember, feel how easy it is for you to go back in time. To remember when you first arrived on this planet, to remember the joy you felt at having the opportunity to contribute, to love, to share, and to help others. *I give myself permission to trust.* As you trust this new feeling unfolding within you, feel how easy it is to know you're right where you need to be.

As you allow for the unfolding of this new energy to embrace you and to envelope you with riches, see yourself standing in line in front of a beautiful white light. Feel this white light drawing you in. The feeling of love is beginning to surround you. Feel the crown of your head beginning to vibrate, to tickle, and allow your true nature to be revealed. *I give myself permission to let go of fear.* As you let go of any fear of manipulation, ugliness, or the unknown, it's important for you to know that you are in control. You have the ability to stop, walk away, or choose a new promise. *I give myself permission to enjoy the process of self-discovery.* As you allow your crown to open and your body to relax, feel this white light coming down from overhead. Feel yourself connecting with the presence of love and removing doubt. Only trust remains. *I give myself permission to experience a new life.* As you give yourself permission to experience a new life, see this path being opened up before you. See the details of your life unfold, feel the importance of making changes, the importance of being clear, the importance of being strong yet gentle, loving yet committed, heartfelt yet bold. *I give myself permission to see my life before me.* As you allow the part of your life that needs your promises to be revealed without fear or anguish, feel yourself being drawn to that part of your life now. See the procedures that are needed, the information that has yet to be revealed; feel yourself opening up to a new mind-set. *I give myself permission to trust the answers I will be given.* As you give yourself permission to trust the answers, feel yourself being drawn into a new paradigm of living. *I give myself permission to excel on all levels: mental, physical, spiritual, and developmental.*

As you give yourself permission to trust in your ability to know what to do and how to do it, see yourself no longer struggling with the mundane. No longer struggling with the small details of life, rather embracing the challenges with enthusiasm and excitement. *I give myself permission to lead by example.* As you give yourself permission to be a leader and to cause new information to spring forth around you, see how easy it is to create breakthrough knowledge, information, awareness, and sustenance simultaneously in your life. *I give myself permission to reveal light.* As you give yourself permission to reveal the light of the Creator, see how easy it is for you to remember the very first promise you made—the promise to reveal your true nature, to allow it to unfold on a path unique to you. *I give myself permission to choose this path again, now, in the way, shape, and form that I am now directed.*

Just as we may all take detours in life, change our minds, or allow circumstances to derail us, feel yourself letting go of what life was supposed to look like, letting go of fear of never being on top again, of never being loved again or never having a true love. *I give myself permission to let go of dead weight.* Give yourself permission to let go at a cellular level of all the thoughts, behaviors, ideas, and insecurities that no longer serve you. *I give myself permission to fly.* As you open your heart, see yourself taking off with a new, expanded awareness of the universe, of how things work, and how you play a vital role in the Creator's plan. Feel how easy it is to trust. How easy it is to give and allow. How easy it is to speak up and share. *I give myself permission to become known.* As you give yourself permission to become known, feel yourself excelling as your strengths are being seen by others and your weaknesses fall away. *I give myself permission to reveal my gifts in the world.* To stand tall, to promise to love and serve, and to be loved for the support and connection of your soul to all living things. *I promise to uncover and rediscover my gifts now. I give myself permission to reveal my promises.* As you give yourself permission to reveal your promises, see yourself letting go of time constraints, of the idea of how long it takes to create miracles or to bring two parties together for the greater good. *I give myself permission to trust the unknown.* As you let go of timelines, of how it needs to look or how you are to get it done, feel yourself simply going to work now. Write down all of the ideas, dreams, inspirations, and thoughts that flood you; allow yourself to bring into focus what you are to see, hear, and know. *I give myself permission to trust.* As you trust this space now, remain in silent meditation for two more minutes and then begin to write what you have seen or heard.

CHAPTER 9

Just Breathe!

Exhale; close your eyes. Notice your body and any tightness, stress, pain, heaviness, whether you're cold or hot. Simply take note of it in your mind.

Put your chin down toward your chest, close your eyes, and pretend that you can see through your chest and that you discover a beautiful butterfly of white light. Then see this butterfly flying down through your chest, down through your legs, ever so gracefully out the bottom of your feet, making a huge tunnel of white light behind it, traveling to what you perceive is the center of the earth. You have followed this butterfly all the way here. Notice that there is a beautiful crystal-clear, blue pool of water here that you can see yourself in. You now imagine the butterfly diving into the pool. You immediately follow her, and while doing so you feel all the grunge, debris, and heaviness fall from you, going deeper and deeper into the crystal-clear pool. Notice how you can breathe in this pool of water; there is no struggle or effort here. Pause and enjoy the moment. Then follow the butterfly back up the tunnel of white light, back up into the bottom of your feet, up through your chest. Feel your body expanding, feel your shoulders relaxing. Continue following this butterfly up and down this tunnel of light and into the pool for at least three breaths, exhaling on the way down and inhaling on the way up. Slow and methodical. Please continue this for three inhalations and three exhalations.

Now, notice how your body feels. You should feel more bottom-heavy, more "together," and more quiet or calm.

Metamorphosis

As you close your eyes and let go of insecurity and fear, feel how easy it is to trust yourself. You may be unable to discern what it is you should be doing at this time in your life. Where do you belong? Know that these feelings of helplessness and insecurity stem from old frequencies that are no longer valuable to you. They were a necessary part in getting you to escape an old path that now no longer serves you. As you are now ready to move forward to receive renewed energies of enlightenment for your highest good on the path that you were meant to live, it is important for you to let go now. Please repeat the following phrase out loud: "I give myself permission to succeed."

While you may already be ready and able to succeed, there seems to be a bit of a challenge in discerning what it is you should succeed at. It is important to let go of these fears and inhibitions now. View your life as if it is part of a large tapestry. See in your mind now this beautiful woven rug: the ends of the rug are frayed and falling apart, but it doesn't keep you from seeing the beauty or the loving touch of the creator of this majestic rug—the love; the devotion it took to create, first in the mind of the master weaver, what outline, forms, and colors, what pattern this rug was to have. Then the diligence, the gentle crafting and weaving, the daily patience it took to follow it through. Know it is in your highest good to say the following words: *I give myself permission to accept what is.*

As you give yourself permission to accept what is, see how easy it is for you to trust, how easy it is for you to know that this rug is safe and secure, that it can take you wherever you want to go, regardless of how tattered and torn it may feel or you may feel. Many times in our lives we are exhausted and no longer want to have to figure things out—we simply want to be told what to do.

I give myself permission to listen to my inner voice. As you give yourself permission to trust your instincts, see now how clearly things come into focus. See yourself stepping up on this magic carpet. As you do so, you notice that it holds your weight; you feel the tightness of the woven thread beneath your hands and legs, the scratchiness of the material, yet there is comfort in this, a simplicity in knowing that you are worth your weight in gold. As you drop your nervousness and settle in, you may now decide to lie upon this gilded mat and to rest, letting go of the worries and strains of parenthood, or caring for an aging parent, or figuring out the bills or how to earn a living, or wondering if you'll ever find that true soul mate or if you'll ever look and feel your best. You may have health issues that are frightening; see this magic carpet as all-inclusive; one that can carry you away from fears, resentments, bitterness, and fatigue; one that can restore you to optimum health.

I give myself permission to rest. As you rest now and you see yourself floating off to sleep, the carpet magically begins to move on the right path, moving, swaying ever so gently, no longer using caution, but confidence, no longer exhibiting anxiety, but patience and fortitude. Feel the strength of this carpet beginning to multiply and to vibrate. The amazing fibers of its core begin to dance around you. You gently place a free hand on your stomach, or solar plexus, now. If you have a specific ailment, place your hand upon this body part now.

I give myself permission to let go of fear. As you release the fear of the unknown adventures that lie ahead, see how easy it is for you to trust, how easy it is for you to take one day at a time, one hour at a time, one moment at a time. In each and every moment lies a breath and ray of light, shafts so clear, so strong, and so enveloping that you want for nothing. All your needs are met; your loneliness subsides; all your desire to be the best or greatest relaxes into a new trust, one of safety and confidence, one of self-assuredness and compassion. Compassion for individuals who cannot, no matter what, accept the inevitable; compassion for those who are so guarded they can't even accept a helping hand or a smile. What has happened to you to make you so cynical that you cannot even enjoy a ride on a magic carpet without getting irritated? Has your life become so filled with yourself, your own ideas, that you cannot let go for even a minute to trust someone else's guidance, to allow someone to help you or assist you? Are you so afraid of being brainwashed that you are paralyzed with fear?

Let go now and trust. Trust that you are in control at all times; trust that you are able to make your own decisions, that you are able to come to your own conclusions, that you are in control of your life and together we are one. Together you and the master weaver will ascend to expanded boundaries. Together this spiritual icon will awaken within you a new sense of self, one that has been dormant for a very long time—a part of you that is now ready to be resurrected to a new sense of security, to move forward with love, adoration, and self-acceptance, first for yourself and then for those around you.

As you now breathe in this beautiful, transparent white light, feel the strength it has. Do not be fooled by its transparency; it is stronger than the strongest fiber on earth. It has more elasticity than the imagination can view. It has more endurance than anything you can ever imagine or touch. Inhale this treasure, accept it as your own. As you smell the burlap and as you accept the presence of life within you, notice that the carpet is now beginning to ascend to a new terrain. Notice this terrain is land, in a field, near a barn: notice the straw, the animals, and the countryside. It feels foreign to you, yet comforting.

As you gently step off the tapestry you notice a small calf nursing from its mother, observe the gentleness and trusting energy that this calf displays, an eagerness to drink from its mother and a feeling of closeness— acknowledge the reality that you didn't arrive at this moment in your life by yourself, that you did have help, no matter in how small an amount, whether it was a parent, a friend, or a teacher who provided a small ray of light somewhere along this line. And whether you choose to disagree, or whether you notice that the ray of light came from yourself, nonetheless you have this ray of light. As you see it reflecting off of this small animal's face, you feel the sincerity and helplessness it has to offer. You notice the gentleness of the breeze.

Or it may be that, at this moment, you only notice what is wrong with life. You focus more on the stench of the barnyard than the beauty that lies before you. Why does your mind work in this fashion? Why do you jump ahead with impatience and frustration? As you let go of your inability to follow along, simply notice that you like things stirred up, that you simply are more inclined to notice the manure than to notice a calf feeding from its mother, having all of its needs met. There is nothing wrong with this mind-set, unless you fight against it.

I give myself permission to surrender to the unknown. As you give yourself permission to let go and to trust, see how easy it is for you to play along, to notice the bullshit and in spite of it smile, in spite of it move forward, in spite of it be successful. As you do, an inward glow appears, a knowing that you did it all by yourself, a knowing that while others may have contributed, you took the time to have patience, to acknowledge others when need be, to spread the glory, to accept the unknown, and to have faith in yourself. So as you gather your belongings and you move forward to a more peaceful terrain, you again are uplifted by the strength of the beautiful woven mat. As it gently lifts up and away from this green setting, you let out a sigh of relief. You maintain your balance, you keep your sense of humor, and you continue forward. As this magic carpet quickly approaches the serenity of city lights, dusk has fallen. It must be a holiday, as traffic is silenced; you see it, but you do not hear it; you notice people along the way frustrated with their lives, yet you feel unaffected. You smile and send them peace; they do not even stop their bickering to notice. You offer a silent prayer for those who do not yet understand that they are in control—control of their circumstances, control of their emotions, and control of their environments.

While this may seem incredible to you, it is the utmost, purest truth. You have all the control. All you need to do is surrender to it. Once you surrender to all of the circumstances and events of your life, the body relaxes and the mind settles, life slows down, a new peace is found, restorative energy is felt. You are now at your core, the core of your beliefs, your wants, and your desires. *I give myself permission to explore my options.* You may be so bent on keeping all of your options open that you cannot commit. Not to your family, not to your work, not to yourself. Release this energy now. Exhale. *I give myself permission to be focused.* As you focus on new ideas, new aspects of your consciousness, feel a new you emerging, one that is strong, tall, and authentic. Not one that duplicates another's actions, not saying things because you think someone wants to hear those things, but a real, genuine you. A new consciousness that is clear.

As you lie back on this beautiful mat, notice it has turned from burlap into velvet and, no matter how hot the day, it is cool to your touch, enveloping you in a beautiful aura of purple strength. As you inhale this vibrant color of purple, the mind shuts off, the body relaxes. The logic stops. You do not need to know how this works; all you need is to trust. As the mind opens and the body communicates perfectly with the mind, feel yourself coming together in a new fashion. Feel the merging of the mind-body connection. Release any inhibitions, any values that no longer serve you, any insecurity that is holding you back.

As the heart opens, a beautiful ray of light comes down from the sky and sheds therapeutic ringlets of green light upon your chest. Rest. Breathe. Enjoy. You are safe. You are at your core. As you are now ushered into a new room, you gently stop and get off the master weaver's rug. You look around the room and are confronted with old filing cabinets, an old storage room. There is dust everywhere, and you have not visited here in a very long time. As you look around the room, you inhale, but none of the dust particles touch your lungs. A beautiful, angelic creature greets you. It is not an ordinary creature; it is a vision of yourself, and one that you recognize, one that you understand, one that you know you are meant to be. It is a smarter, more peaceful version of you. You can feel the confidence, the strength, and the compassion of this being. The knowing, the understanding, the purpose of this being. You recognize to your core what you have been lacking. You see it clearly in your own face and you receive it now. Your arms relax; your body opens up to this new realization that you have known all along. That you are safe, whole, and complete. That you are and will always be in control, that your sense of humor, peace of mind, fortitude, love, and devotion will enable you to move forward with purpose and insight. *I accept my calling now.*

Magically this figure goes to work, bringing out old dead files that are no longer used or needed. Some apply to you, some apply to your friends or family members, some apply to others in the world, but nonetheless you witness transformation now. You notice the names on these files as they are quickly pulled and dropped at your feet. *I'm angry, I can't be trusted, I'm a liar and a thief, I'm a drunk, I'm a whore, I'm a rapist, I'm scared. I'm a victim,*

I'm a drug user, I'm a loner, and I don't need your help. I don't need your friendship. I'm angry, I'm bored, I'm forgetful, I'm lazy, I'm stupid, I'm fat, I'm insincere. I'm in it for the money. I want to die, I'm afraid. All these files pile up and drop beneath your feet. Your body releases any recognition of past lives or of present memories associated with any beliefs that no longer serve you. Your mind opens a shaft and small raisins begin to drop out, little pellets of darkness that never came to fruition: fruit that could not be used, wine that could not be drunk, songs that could not be sung because of these old dying ugly beliefs that have been left on the planet. *I am free.*

As the mind opens up and you begin to wander, allow for a new room to appear. Magically the room is cleared and clean, magically the filing cabinets are gone, and you are suspended in an air of confidence. The beautiful angel has shifted from what you perceived to be you to a new guide. An angelic face looks back at you. You may recognize it, you may not. You accept its love now. *I open my heart to love.* A beautiful pink light fills all the dark holes in your mind, the places where old beliefs were lodged. Your body relaxes, your mind opens up, and you receive the pink shafts of light dancing throughout your entire midsection, going from toe to toe, dancing from ear to ear, covering each and every cell until you feel your entire body dancing and vibrating with beautiful, electric pink light. It expands beyond your body and beyond your mind, flooding the room.

You slowly, gently see the tapestry in your mind. It is now whole and complete, just as the Creator intended. There are no holes left to fill, it is no longer tattered or rough; it is smooth, opulent, soft and yet sturdy. There is a serenity and peaceful inner strength associated with this beautiful masterpiece. You gently touch the rug. It is now soft as a baby's blanket. You roll it up, you wrap it around you, and you touch it to your face. You are home, safe, sound, and secure. You are at peace. You have no worries or insecurities. You know what to do, your purpose is emerging in your view, and you are calm. It comes to you magically, the next step. You relax, you trust, you move forward. *I am safe.*

Continue to breathe slowly, and when you're ready, start to wiggle your toes, stretch your fingers, roll your shoulders, and move your body to whatever position feels comfortable, slowly coming back and waking up. Exhale. Just take your time.

Write down your number (from 1 to 5). Then go on to write anything you felt or saw during this meditation that you feel is important to you, any messages you may have received. Then go to your corresponding number below to anchor your experience; first by repeating the phrase out loud and then by breathing in the designated color. Repeat three times a day for three days for optimal results.

ANCHORING AND LIGHT WORK

Mantras and Colors

1. I am safe, secure, and able to complete my duties efficiently and impeccably. I am rested. My mind and body no longer compete. Optimal health is mine. I surrender to the unknown. I am at peace. *Color: green.*

2. I receive love easily and effortlessly from those around me. I clearly speak my truth with confidence, ease, and gratitude. I welcome new life adventures that support who I am in the world. I am at peace. I am shown and recognize the way. *Colors: yellow and blue.*

3. I easily gather support for ideas that bring about awareness, truth, and clarity. I stand tall in my truth with love and conviction. I am free to be me. *Color: yellow.*

4. I acknowledge truth; I accept my calling now; and I am sincere, confident, and abundant in riches of the heart. I release wounds of the heart and welcome peace to my soul. I breathe in life's riches easily; I move forward easily. It's safe to see. *Color: red.*

5. I'm supported, loved, and contrite. I release bitterness and anger through writing. I accept my calling to a more peaceful life now. I deserve all good things. I open my heart to love. *Color: white.*

ACKNOWLEDGMENTS

To my parents, Alvin and Colletta Rottinghaus, for their unwavering faith, strength, and unconditional love, which they have exhibited to me throughout this process of discovering my gifts. Thank you for being such wonderful role models.

To my remaining close-knit siblings, Ron, Mark, and Bill Rottinghaus, and my sister, Sue Reiter, for expressing their care and concern for me during the difficult paths of learning I went through. Thanks for making me stronger.

To my children, Marco, Renzo, and Risa Rometo, for loving me for who I am and doing their best to keep me "normal." I'm so proud of all of you.

To my fabulous husband, Bob, of 20 plus years, for his passion and deep belief that I have been given something special to share with the world and who has taught me how to believe in myself. You're my rock.

I love you all and feel blessed to be part of such an amazing family.

There have been so many special people throughout the years who have helped me and encouraged me to find my voice in the world. Healers Marilyn Overcast & David Cunningham, who helped me make sense of the phenomena I was experiencing. My cousin Julie Dunnwald, Ph.D., who held my hand, calmed my fears, and kept me grounded when I had no clue what that meant. Linda Ratto and Jan Corrali, who so many years ago both poured their heart and soul into helping me hone my message. Thank you all for your generosity. Anne Barthel for making sense of my ramblings and the cacophony of voices that initially haunted my pages. You are amazing!

To Louise Hay and Reid Tracy, for taking a chance on me; and to my fabulous editor, Patty Gift, for celebrating me throughout the long, arduous process of grooming a first-time author. Hay House is the best because of you!

To my good friend and literary agent, Cynthia Cannell, whose tireless efforts, impeccability, brilliance, and savvy business sense helped me guide this book to my dream publisher, Hay House. Your constant source of encouragement and tenacity kept me on track. Thank you for your wisdom, unending friendship, support, and love. I'm grateful for the bond we share, and I look forward to our next adventure.

I've had the privilege of meeting a few of the world's most famous women who've broken through the glass ceiling in their profession and paved the way for the rest of us.

It's rare to meet people you idolize only to discover that everything wonderful that the world has said about them is true. That's how I feel about these women, beginning with my dear friend Demi Moore. She is one of the most compassionate, talented, intelligent, fun-loving, and loyal individuals I know. She has a huge heart and isn't afraid to show it. Her friendship and certainty in the early stages of my work gave me the faith and belief in myself to expand my vision of what I thought was possible for me. She is truly a visionary and a remarkable woman.

In addition to Demi, I'm blessed to have amazing friends such as Donna Karan of the fashion industry,

Joni Evans of the publishing industry, and Mary Wells Lawrence of the advertising world. Each has opened doors for me, gifted me with their wisdom, and championed my work. Thank you all for being who you are in the world and sharing your honesty and gifts with me. It's a privilege I don't take lightly. Thank you for being part of my life.

To my first spiritual teacher, Monsignor Edward Petty, of blessed memory, who helped affirm my gift for my family. You were an amazing man and are greatly missed by many. The lineage of great Kabbalists and my teachers at the Kabbalah Center, especially, Yehuda Berg, Shalom Sharabi, and David Ghyiam, whose dedication, guidance, and care inspire me to want to do more for the world. I feel so fortunate to be connected with you. I'm greatly appreciative of my spiritual guides for being a constant source of healing, comfort, and wisdom for myself and others as we strive to become more like the Creator.

Huge hugs of gratitude to my soul sisters, Lynn Burgess and Cheryl Grace, whom I can always count on to pick me up when I am down and who have always given me great heart-felt wisdom.

Special thanks to Judi Cannon, Jeanne Dimidio, and all of my "Peggy's Partners," too numerous to name, who have helped me along the way while infusing me with joy, friendship, and certainty. You know who you are! Finally for all of the individuals that have given me the privilege of sharing my gift with you; namely family and friends who let me "practice" on you in the early years. I hope it wasn't too painful—thank you for your courage! To my precious clients, my second family—some of you I've yet to meet in person—thank you for your faith, trust, and perseverance. You're an inspiration to me. If it weren't for you, none of this would have been possible. I look forward to our continued journey together learning from one another.

With much love and appreciation,
Namaste,
Peggy

ENDNOTES

1. Michael Berg, ed., *The Zohar, Volume 3, Lech Lecha* (Research Center of Kabbalah, May 2000): section 3, page 10.

2. Ibid.

3. Candace Pert, *Molecules of Emotion* (New York: Simon & Schuster, 1999), 269.

4. Psalm 23.

ABOUT THE AUTHOR

Peggy Rometo is a gifted intuitive healer, psychic medium, and Reiki master who counsels people around the world through her workshops, recordings, and personal sessions. She advises her clients, who range from Fortune 500 executives to world-renowned actors to everyday individuals, on a wide array of concerns. Peggy teaches master classes and seminars, and has taught an ongoing class about tapping into your intuition called Bridging the GAP for the past ten years. She is also a weekly contributor to Women on the Web (**www.wowOwow.com**) and a member of a nonprofit panel of psychics who assist law enforcement in finding missing people worldwide with the Find Me organization (**www.FindMe2.com**).

For more information, visit her Website: **www.peggyrometo.com**, or call 941-756-0936.

NOTES

NOTES

NOTES

∽ NOTES ∽

NOTES

NOTES

NOTES

 NOTES

NOTES

❧ NOTES ❧

NOTES

∽ NOTES ∽

∽ NOTES ∽

NOTES

HAY HOUSE TITLES OF RELATED INTEREST

YOU CAN HEAL YOUR LIFE, the movie,
starring Louise L. Hay & Friends
(available as a 1-DVD program and
an expanded 2-DVD set)
Watch the trailer at: **www.LouiseHayMovie.com**

THE SHIFT, the movie,
starring Dr. Wayne W. Dyer
(available as a 1-DVD program and an
expanded 2-DVD set)
Watch the trailer at: **www.DyerMovie.com**

⁓

DEFY GRAVITY: Healing Beyond the Bounds of Reason,
by Caroline Myss

EXCUSES BEGONE!: How to Change Lifelong,
Self-Defeating Thinking Habits, by Dr. Wayne W. Dyer

THE INTUITIVE ADVISOR: A Psychic Doctor Teaches
You How to Solve Your Most Pressing Health Problems,
by Mona Lisa Schulz, M.D., Ph.D.

THE KEYS: Open the Door to True Empowerment and
Infinite Possibilites, by Denise Marek and Sharon Quirt

THE SPIRIT WHISPERER: Chronicles of a Medium,
by John Holland

⁓

All of the above are available at your local bookstore,
or may be ordered by contacting Hay House (see next page).

We hope you enjoyed this Hay House book.
If you'd like to receive our online catalog featuring additional
information on Hay House books and products, or if you'd like to
find out more about the Hay Foundation, please contact:

Hay House, Inc.
P.O. Box 5100
Carlsbad, CA 92018-5100
(760) 431-7695 or **(800) 654-5126**
(760) 431-6948 (fax) or **(800) 650-5115 (fax)**
www.hayhouse.com® • **www.hayfoundation.org**

Published and distributed in Australia by: Hay House Australia Pty.
Ltd., 18/36 Ralph St., Alexandria NSW 2015 • *Phone:* 612-9669-4299
• *Fax:* 612-9669-4144 • www.hayhouse.com.au

Published and distributed in the United Kingdom by: Hay House
UK, Ltd., 292B Kensal Rd., London W10 5BE • *Phone:* 44-20-8962-
1230 • *Fax:* 44-20-8962-1239 • www.hayhouse.co.uk

Published and distributed in the Republic of South Africa by:
Hay House SA (Pty), Ltd., P.O. Box 990, Witkoppen 2068 • *Phone/Fax:*
27-11-467-8904 • info@hayhouse.co.za • www.hayhouse.co.za

Published in India by: Hay House Publishers India, Muskaan
Complex, Plot No. 3, B-2, Vasant Kunj, New Delhi 110 070 • *Phone:*
91-11-4176-1620 • *Fax:* 91-11-4176-1630 • www.hayhouse.co.in

Distributed in Canada by: Raincoast, 9050 Shaughnessy St.,
Vancouver, B.C. V6P 6E5 • Phone: (604) 323-7100
Fax: (604) 323-2600 • www.raincoast.com

Take Your Soul on a Vacation

Visit **www.HealYourLife.com®** to regroup, recharge, and reconnect
with your own magnificence.Featuring blogs, mind-body-spirit
news, and life-changing wisdom from Louise Hay and friends.

Visit **www.HealYourLife.com** today!